AROOSTOOK WAR.

HISTORICAL SKETCH

AND

Roster of Commissioned Officers and Enlisted Men

CALLED INTO SERVICE FOR THE PROTECTION OF THE NORTHEASTERN FRONTIER OF MAINE.

FROM FEBRUARY TO MAY, 1839.

Published in accordance with Council Order passed November 24, 1903.

CLEARFIELD COMPANY
REPRINTS & REMAINDERS

Reprinted for Clearfield Company Inc. by
Genealogical Publishing Co. Inc.
Baltimore, MD 1989

HISTORICAL SKETCH AND ROSTER OF COMMISSIONED OFFICERS AND ENLISTED MEN OF THE DRAFTED MILITIA OF MAINE, CALLED INTO ACTUAL SERVICE FOR THE PROTECTION OF ITS NORTHEASTERN FRONTIER, FROM FEBRUARY TO MAY, 1839.

THE AROOSTOOK WAR, 1839.

Among the many important events in the early history of the State of Maine one of much interest is that known as the Aroostook War, a brief sketch of which is given below.

By the treaty of 1783, at the close of the Revolutionary struggle, one-half of the St. John's river belonged to Maine. * * * After the war of 1812, the British claimed the whole of the upper part of the vast valley of the St. John. They demanded all the land above the forty-sixth degree of north latitude, which included about one-third of what was supposed to be the territory of Maine. There was at this time, on the north or eastern side of the river, an American settlement * * * extending for a distance of nearly twenty miles. The inhabitants were principally of French descent, and had emigrated to that American region when the English took possession of Arcadia. This plantation had been incorporated as the town of Madawaska, and a representative was sent to the legislature of Maine. In June, 1837, Congress sent an officer to Madawaska to take a census of the people, and at the same time to distribute the surplus money which had accumulated in the United States treasury. A British constable arrested this agent and carried his prisoner to the nearest English shire town. But the sheriff there, alarmed, refused to receive the prisoner, and he returned to Madawaska, and continued to prosecute his mission.

Governor Harvey of New Brunswick, hearing of the distribution of money to the people, assumed that it was a bribe to induce the inhabitants to continue their allegiance to the United States. He therefore ordered the agent to be re-arrested and he was lodged in Frederickton jail. Governor Dunlap, at that time governor of Maine, issued a general order announcing that the soil of our State had been invaded by a foreign power. The militia were therefore called upon to hold themselves in readiness for active service. A few weeks after, the British authorities set the imprisoned agent at liberty. Both parties wisely decided to refer the question to arbitration.

By the convention between the United States and Great Britain, at London, September 29, 1827, it was agreed through the plenipotentiaries of the two powers, that points of difference between the commissioners appointed according to the fifth article of the treaty of Ghent, should be referred to some friendly sovereign or state. They finally made a choice of William, King of Netherlands, as arbiter of questions submitted under that treaty.

The question in regard to the northeastern boundary being referred to him, he decided that the line should run about halfway between the boundaries claimed by the two powers.

The question submitted was "Which of the two boundaries is the one authorized by the treaty?" and he decided in favor of a line which the treaty did not indicate, and of which neither of the parties had thought. The people of Maine were indignant at this decision. The national government, anxious to avoid war, generously offered Maine a million acres of land in Michigan, in exchange for the territory she would thus lose. This offer was declined, and prolonged negotiations ensued. During the years from 1832, when the decision was waived by both the interested parties, until 1842, when Maine assented to a compromise, there had been frequent collisions on the frontier. In 1838, Governor Kent took measures to increase the efficiency of the militia, and General Wool was sent to inspect the fortifications on the Penobscot, the St. Croix and the Kennebec. The line which Maine claimed by the treaty of 1783 was again surveyed. The territory thus in dispute became the prey of plunderers. Soon there was a conflict between the British lumbermen and American officers.

Governor Harvey of New Brunswick issued a proclamation declaring that British territory had been invaded and ordering out a thousand of the militia. Affairs now began to look serious. Immediately fifty volunteers set out from Augusta for the scene of action. At the same time Governor Harvey sent a communication to the governor of Maine, at Augusta, demanding the recall of the American troops from the Aroostook, announcing that he was instructed by the British government to hold exclusive charge over the disputed territory and that he should do so by military force. This aroused the indignation of the people of Maine. The legislature passed a resolve for the protection of the public lands, and appropriated eight hundred thousand dollars to that purpose. A draft was also ordered for ten thousand three hundred and forty-three men from the militia to be ready for immediate action. General Bachelder was commander of the western division of militia. Within a week ten thousand American troops were either in Aroostook county, or on the march there. The national government was roused. Congress passed a bill authorizing the President of the United States to raise fifty thousand troops for the support of Maine, and appropriating ten million dollars to meet the expense, should the governor of New Brunswick fulfil his threat of maintaining exclusive jurisdiction over the territory in dispute. On the fifth of March, General Scott with his staff, reached Augusta. He informed the governor that he was "specially charged with maintaining the peace and safety of the entire northern and eastern frontiers." He took quarters at the Augusta House and entered into correspondence with both Governor Harvey of New Brunswick and Governor Fairfield of Maine, endeavoring to act the part of peacemaker.

Governor Harvey pledged himself that, in prospect of the peaceful settlement of the question between the two nations, he would not take military possession of the territory, or endeavor to expel from it the civil posse or the troops of Maine. Governor Fairfield pledged himself that he would not, without renewed instructions, disturb any of the New Brunswick settlements in the Madawaska region. He agreed to withdraw his troops and leave uninterrupted communication between New Brunswick and Canada.

This settlement brought peace. The prisoners on both sides were set at liberty. In March, the Aroostook region, which had previously formed a portion of Penobscot and Washington counties, was formed into a new county bearing its original name. It was generally supposed that the prompt military preparations we had made, which gave us the command of the situation, had great influence with the British authorities in securing a peaceful settlement. Although the Aroostook war called for troops which were sent to the scene of disturbance, the outbreak was a bloodless one; nevertheless it was the occasion of great annoyance and the expenditure of large sums of money.

In the year 1842 Lord Ashburton came to Washington, the British ambassador authorized to form a new treaty for the settlement of the boundary. An extra session of the legislature of Maine was called. Commissioners were appointed to confer with Lord Ashburton and Secretary Webster upon this subject. The troublesome question was soon settled. England greatly needed a portion of this territory that there might be free communication between New Brunswick and Canada. Maine surrendered a considerable tract which was of but little value. In compensation the United States received a territory of much greater value, on the borders of Lakes Champlain and Superior. The national government paid Maine one hundred and fifty thousand dollars for the surrender. The State also received two hundred thousand dollars as re-imbursement for the expense she had incurred in defending the integrity of American territory. The Senate of the United States ratified the Ashburton treaty August 20, 1842. By this treaty, which is sometimes called from the negotiations the Webster-Ashburton treaty, arrangements were made for the final settlement of boundaries between the different states and the British possessions in North America.

Much interesting matter in regard to this subject is found in "Abbott's History of Maine." The printed volumes of "Resolves of the State of Maine" contain valuable material connected with those years of open controversy. Other works are by Albert Gallatin, "The Right of the United States to the Northeastern Boundary Claimed by Them," (New York, 1840); Chas. S. Daveis "Report of the Committee on the North Eastern Boundary, Legislative Documents, 1841;" William P. Preble "The Decision of the King of Netherlands" published anonymously, (Portland, 1841).

Following are general orders issued in 1839, which relate to the Aroostook War, also a list of officers in active service at that time and the muster rolls of forty-six companies of infantry and artillery which were called into active service.

STATE OF MAINE.
HEADQUARTERS,
AUGUSTA, February 16, 1839.

General Order, No. 5.

Major General Isaac Hodsdon, third Division, Maine Militia:—You are hereby ordered to detach, forthwith, from the Division under your command, by draft or otherwise one thousand men, properly officered and equipped. This force will rendezvous at Bangor and proceed at the earliest possible moment, to the place occupied by a civil force under the Land Agent on or near the Aroostook river, and render such aid to the Land Agent as may enable him to carry into effect a Resolve of 24th of January, relating to trespassers upon the public lands.

(Signed)   JOHN FAIRFIELD,
Gov. and Commander-in-Chief.

STATE OF MAINE.
HEADQUARTERS,
AUGUSTA, February 17, 1839.

General Order, No. 6.

Major General Hodsdon of the third Division, having been directed by General Orders of the 16th instant, to make a draft of one thousand men from his Division, the detailment will consist of eight hundred and fifty Infantry, Light Infantry and Riflemen, and one hundred and fifty Artillery. The companies will be organized with sixty-four privates, four sergeants, and two musicians. The draft will be required to report themselves to the Major General at Bangor, on Thursday the 21st instant. The Major General will command the detachment in person, and he will detail, in addition to the proper number of Company officers, one Colonel, one Lieutenant Colonel, and one Major of Infantry, and one Major of Artillery, together with the appropriate Staff. General Hodsdon will make immediate requisition by express on the acting Quartermaster General, for such supplies, including military stores, as in his opinion, the nature of the service contemplated may require.

The detachment will be required to appear with the arms and equipments of their respective corps, and with three days' provisions. They will be drafted to serve three months unless sooner discharged.

When the detachment shall have been completed, Major General Hodsdon will forward to the Adjutant General a complete roll of the officers, non-commissioned officers and privates, describing the Brigade, Regiment and Companies from which they were severally taken.

General Hodsdon will procure at Bangor, or at such other place as he may find convenient, the necessary camp equipage for the detachment.
By the Commander-in-Chief.
(Signed) A. B. THOMPSON,
Adj. Genl.

STATE OF MAINE.
HEADQUARTERS,
AUGUSTA, February 19, 1839.

General Order, No. 7.

The Commander-in-Chief directs a detachment of ten thousand three hundred and forty-three officers, non-commissioned officers and privates, including field and staff officers, to be made by draft from the several Divisions, in the proportions, and from the several corps mentioned in the schedule of detail prepared by the Adjutant General. The officers and soldiers when detached will severally hold themselves in readiness for an immediate call into the service of the State, armed and equipped as required by law.

The Major Generals and officers commanding Divisions are directed to cause the draft aforesaid, to be made with all possible expedition, and complete rolls of both officers and men, designating the Companies, Regiments and Brigades from which they are taken, to be immediately forwarded to the office of the Adjutant General.

In making this call upon a portion of the military force, to hold itself in readiness for active service, the Commander-in-Chief would remind the whole body of the militia, of the important position they occupy as citizen soldiers; and should the contingency unfortunately occur, when their services should be required to render protection to our citizens, or preserve the honor of our State, he will rely with entire confidence on their patriotism for such aid as the exigency may require.

By the Commander-in-Chief.
(Signed) A. B. THOMPSON,
Adjutant General.

STATE OF MAINE.
ADJUTANT GENERAL'S OFFICE,
AUGUSTA, Feb. 19, 1839.

The following is the detail of the detachment made pursuant to the foregoing General Order, numbered 7, and of this date:

AROOSTOOK WAR. 9

CAVALRY.

Division.	Captain.	Lieutenants.	Cornets.	Sergeants.	Musicians.	Privates.	Total.
2	1	-	-	1	1	20	23
3	-	1	-	2	-	20	23
8	-	1	1	1	1	24	28
	1	2	1	4	2	64	74

ARTILLERY.

Division.	Colonels.	Lieut. Cols.	Majors.	Adjutants.	Quartermasters.	Paymasters.	Chaplains.	Surgeons.	Surg. Mates.	Sergt. Major.	Q. M. Sergt.	Drum Major.	Fife Major.	Captains.	Lieutenants.	Sergeants.	Drummers.	Fifers.	Privates.	Total.
1	-	-	1	-	-	-	1	-	-	1	1	-	-	-	1	3	-	1	30	35
2	-	-	1	-	-	-	1	-	-	1	1	-	-	1	1	2	1	1	60	70
3	-	-	-	-	-	-	-	-	-	-	-	-	-	-	2	2	1	1	24	30
4	-	1	-	-	1	1	-	-	-	-	-	1	-	1	2	4	1	1	80	93
5	-	-	-	-	-	-	-	-	-	-	-	-	-	1	1	2	1	-	34	39
6	-	-	-	-	-	-	-	-	-	-	-	-	-	1	2	4	1	-	40	48
7	-	-	-	1	-	-	-	-	-	-	-	-	-	1	1	3	-	1	36	42
8	1	-	-	1	-	-	-	1	1	-	-	-	1	1	2	4	1	1	80	94
	1	1	1	1	1	1	1	1	1	1	1	1	1	6	12	24	6	6	384	451

INFANTRY.

Division.	Colonel.	Lieut. Cols.	Majors.	Adjutants.	Quar. Masters.	Pay Masters.	Chaplains.	Surgeons.	Surg. Mates.	Sergt. Majors.	Q. M. Sergts.	Drum Major.	Fife Major.	Captains.	Lieutenants.	Engigns.	Sergeants.	Drummers.	Fifers.	Privates.	Total.
1	2	2	2	2	2	2	2	2	2	2	2	2	2	15	16	16	60	16	16	1,000	1,165
2	2	2	2	2	2	2	2	2	2	2	2	2	2	16	15	16	64	16	16	1,000	1,169
3	1	2	2	1	1	1	1	1	1	1	1	1	1	8	8	8	32	8	8	500	587
4	2	3	2	2	2	2	2	2	2	2	2	2	2	16	16	15	64	15	15	1,000	1,168
5	2	1	2	2	2	2	2	2	2	2	2	2	2	12	12	12	48	12	12	750	883
6	2	1	1	2	2	2	2	2	2	2	2	2	2	12	12	12	48	12	12	750	883
7	1	1	1	1	1	1	1	1	1	1	1	1	1	9	9	9	36	9	9	600	694
8	2	1	2	2	2	2	2	2	2	2	2	2	2	12	12	12	48	12	12	800	933
	14	14	14	14	14	14	14	14	14	14	14	14	14	100	100	100	400	100	100	6,400	7,482

LIGHT INFANTRY.

Division.	Captain.	Lieutenant.	Ensign.	Sergeant.	Drummer.	Fifes.	Private.	Total.
1	2	2	2	8	2	2	126	144
2	3	3	3	12	3	3	200	227
3	3	4	3	12	3	3	230	258
4	4	4	4	16	4	4	250	286
5	5	4	4	20	5	5	300	343
6	3	3	3	12	3	3	180	207
7	1	1	2	4	1	1	50	60
8	3	3	3	12	3	3	200	227
	24	24	24	96	24	24	1,536	1,752

RIFLEMEN.

Division.	Captain.	Lieutenant.	Ensigns.	Sergeants.	Drummers.	Fifers.	Privates.	Total.
2	2	2	1	6	2	2	100	115
3	1	1	1	5	1	1	80	90
4	1	1	2	5	1	1	80	91
5	1	1	2	5	1	1	80	91
6	2	1	1	5	1	2	92	104
7	-	1	-	2	1	-	20	24
8	1	1	1	4	1	1	60	69
	8	8	8	32	8	8	512	584

RECAPITULATION.

Division.	Cavalry.	Artillery.	Infantry.	Light Infantry.	Riflemen.	Total.
1	-	35	1,165	144	-	1,134
2	23	70	1,169	227	115	1,604
3	23	30	587	258	90	988
4	-	93	1,168	286	91	1,638
5	-	39	883	343	91	1,356
6	-	48	883	207	104	1,242
7	-	42	694	60	24	820
8	28	94	933	227	69	1,351
	74	451	7,482	1,752	584	10,343

(Signed)   A. B. THOMPSON,
Adjutant General.

STATE OF MAINE.

HEADQUARTERS,
AUGUSTA, Feb. 22, 1839.

General Order, No. 10.

Brigadier General George W. Bachelder, of the first Brigade of the second Division, will forthwith repair to Headquarters and report himself to the Adjutant General, and wait orders for special duty.

The detachment made from the first Brigade of the second Division, pursuant to General Order number seven of February 19, 1839, excepting Cavalry, is ordered into the service of the State. The detachment will be forthwith organized into Companies, consisting as nearly as may be, of sixty-four privates, four sergeants and two musicians, and will assemble at the Court House in Augusta on Monday the twenty-fifth day of February, instant, at nine o'clock in the forenoon, with the arms and equipments of their respective corps, including knapsacks and blankets, required by law for actual service. Each man will furnish himself with three days' provisions; and officers commanding Regiments will forthwith notify the selectmen of towns, to cause the detachment from their respective towns to be attended on their march with suitable carriages, provisions, camp equipage and camp utensils, until notice shall be given them by the commanding officers to desist.

Upon the arrival of the several Companies at Augusta, each commanding officer thereof will report himself to Brigadier General Bachelder, together with the state of his Company.

The field and staff officers of the detachment will also report themselves to Brigadier General Bachelder at the time appointed.

The detachment aforesaid will serve for the term of three months, unless sooner discharged by the Commander-in-Chief.

Major General White will detail one Brigade Major, one Aid de Camp to Brigadier General and one Brigade Quartermaster, for the staff of Brigadier General Bachelder, and the officers detailed will be required to report themselves to him at Augusta, at the time appointed for the rendezvous of the detachment.

By the Commander-in-Chief.
(Signed) A. B. THOMPSON,
Adj. Genl.

STATE OF MAINE.

HEADQUARTERS,
AUGUSTA, February 22, 1839.

General Order, No. 11.

Major General Ezekiel Foster of the seventh Division, will order into the service of the State, from that portion of his Division directed by General Order number seven of February 19, 1839, to be held in readiness for a call, excepting therefrom those residing in the town of Calais, four

Captains, four Lieutenants, four Ensigns, sixteen sergeants, eight musicians, and two hundred and fifty-six privates of Infantry; and one Captain, one Lieutenant, one Ensign, four sergeants, two musicians and sixty-four privates of Light Infantry. The detachment will be immediately organized into Companies of sixty-four privates, four sergeants and two musicians, and they will be required to march forthwith to the town of Calais. They will be retained in service three months, unless sooner discharged by the Commander-in-Chief.

The necessary orders will be given for the troops to provide themselves with arms and equipment complete for active service, and three days' rations, and also for the commanding officers of Regiments to give notice to the selectmen to provide suitable carriages, provisions, camp equipage and camp utensils, while on the march, until notified to desist.

Major General Foster will himself proceed to Calais in due season, with two members of his staff, and take immediate command of the troops ordered out.

General Foster will make immediate requisition on the acting Quartermaster General, for such supplies, including military stores, as he may deem necessary—which requisition will be presented to Captain Randall Whidden of Calais, and Captain of the Calais Artillery, who will take immediate measures to answer the call. He will also forward complete rolls of both officers and men, designating the Companies, Regiments and Brigades from which they were taken, to the office of the Adjutant General.

By the Commander-in-Chief.
    (Signed)   A. B. THOMPSON,
                         Adj. Genl.

STATE OF MAINE.
HEADQUARTERS,
AUGUSTA, February 27, 1839.
General Order, No. 12.

The Commander-in-Chief directs that there be immediately called into the service of the State, by detail and draft, from the detachment made pursuant to General Order, No. 7, of February 19, 1839, the following officers, non-commissioned officers and privates, viz:—

From the Fourth Division, one Quartermaster and one Paymaster of Artillery; from the Fifth Division, two Captains, two Lieutenants, two Ensigns, eight Sergeants, two Drummers, two Fifers, and one hundred and twenty-eight privates of Light Infantry; one Captain, one Lieutenant, one Ensign, four Sergeants, one Drummer, one Fifer, and sixty-four privates of Riflemen; from the Sixth Division, one Lieutenant Colonel, one Major, one Adjutant, one Quartermaster, one Paymaster, one Chaplain, one Surgeon, one Surgeon's mate, one Sergeant Major, one Quartermaster Sergeant, one Drum Major, one Fife Major, four Captains, four Lieutenants, four Ensigns, sixteen Sergeants, four Drummers, four Fifers, and two hundred and fifty-six privates of Infantry; one Captain, one Lieutenant, one Ensign, four Sergeants, one Drummer, one Fifer, and sixty-four privates of Riflemen; and from the Eighth Division, one Lieutenant Colonel, one Major, one Adjutant, one Quartermaster, one Paymaster, one Chaplain, one Surgeon, one Surgeon's mate, one Sergeant Major, one Quartermaster Sergeant, one Drum Major, one Fife Major, four Captains, four Lieutenants, four Ensigns, sixteen Sergeants, four Drummers, four Fifers, and two hundred and fifty-six privates of Infantry; and one Adjutant, one Captain, two Lieutenants, four Sergeants, one Drummer, one Fifer, and sixty-four privates of Artillery. Major Generals will cause this draft to be immediately organized into Companies of four Sergeants, one Drummer, one Fifer, and sixty-four privates, and will cause them to rendezvous as follows:

Those from the Fifth Division, at the Court House in Portland, on Monday the fourth day of March next, at nine o'clock in the forenoon, and they will report themselves to Major General Jewett, who will place them under command of the senior Captain of the draft, with orders to proceed forthwith to Augusta and report his command at Headquarters, to the Adjutant General.

Those from the Sixth Division at the Court House in Augusta, on Wednesday the sixth day of March next, at nine o'clock in the forenoon, and report themselves by commanding officers of Companies to the Adjutant General at Headquarters.

Those from the Eighth Division, at the Inn of Dudley Heywood in Skowhegan, on Tuesday the twelfth day of March next, at nine o'clock in the forenoon, and report themselves to Major General Bodfish, who will place them under command of Colonel Nathan Goodridge, with orders to proceed on the road to Bangor, subject to the further orders of the Commander-in-Chief.

The Quartermaster and Paymaster from the Fourth Division, will report themselves to the Adjutant General at Headquarters, on Wednesday the sixth day of March next, at nine o'clock in the forenoon.

All the troops aforesaid will appear at their several places of rendezvous, with the arms and equipments of their respective corps, including knapsacks and blankets, required by law for actual service. Each man will furnish himself with three days' provisions; and officers commanding Regiments and Battalions will forthwith notify the selectmen of towns, to cause the detachment from their respective towns to be attended on their march with suitable carriages, provisions, camp equipage and camp utensils, until notice shall be given them by the commanding officer to desist.

Major Generals will forward complete rolls of both officers and men, designating the Companies, Regiments and Brigades from which they were taken, to the office of the Adjutant General, with all possible dispatch.

The several field and staff officers of the draft, from the Sixth Division, will report themselves with the other troops from their Division to the Adjutant General at Headquarters; and those from the Eighth Division, will report themselves with the troops from that Division to Major General Bodfish, who will organize his draft into a Regiment.

The detachment hereby called into service, will serve for the term of three months, unless sooner discharged by the Commander-in-Chief.

Colonel Orison Ripley of the First Regiment, First Brigade and Sixth Division, is ordered into service, and he will report himself to the Adjutant General at Headquarters, on Monday the fourth day of March next, at nine o'clock in the forenoon, and await orders.

Colonel Nathan Goodridge of the First Regiment, Second Brigade, and Eighth Division, is ordered into service, and he will report himself to his Major General, at Skowhegan, on Tuesday the twelfth day of March next, at nine o'clock in the forenoon and await orders.

By the Commander-in-Chief.

A. B. THOMPSON,
Adjutant General.

STATE OF MAINE.
HEADQUARTERS,
AUGUSTA, February 27, 1839.

General Order, No. 13.

General Order, No. 12 of this date is so far altered, as to permit Major General Jewett of the Fifth Division, to receive the "A" Company of Light Infantry, and the "A" Company of Riflemen, both in the Third Regiment of the Second Brigade in said Division, with the several officers, sergeants, one drummer and one fifer, and all the privates not exceeding sixty-four in number, in each company, as a part of the draft ordered from his Division, by General Order, No. 12; and to complete the number required by said General Order, he will make regular detail and draft from the detachment made pursuant to General Order, No. 7, of February 19, 1839.

By the Commander-in-Chief.

A. B. THOMPSON,
Adjutant General.

STATE OF MAINE.
HEADQUARTERS,
AUGUSTA, March 1, 1839.

General Order, No. 15.

Major General Alvan Bolster of the Sixth Division, will immediately order into the service of the State from his Division, in addition to the detachment directed by General Order, No. 12, of February 27, 1839, four Captains, four Lieutenants, four Ensigns, sixteen Sergeants, four Drummers, four Fifers, and two hundred and fifty-six privates of Infantry; one Captain, two Lieutenants, four Sergeants, one Drummer, one Fifer and sixty-four privates of Artillery; and one Captain, one Lieutenant, one Ensign, four Sergeants, one Drummer, one Fifer and sixty-four privates of Light Infantry.

This additional draft will be armed, provided for in every respect, and rendezvous, as mentioned in General Order, No. 12, for the detachment in the Sixth Division, and remain in service three months; unless sooner discharged by the Commander-in-Chief. General Bolster will cause the Company of Artillery to be properly armed for field duty.

By the Commander-in-Chief.

A. B. THOMPSON,
Adj. Genl.

STATE OF MAINE.

HEADQUARTERS,
AUGUSTA, February 28, 1839.

General Order, No. 16.

On the mustering of any detachment of troops ordered into the service of the State, at the place of rendezvous, should there be any material deficiency of able-bodied officers or men, the officer ordered to command such detachment will forthwith notify the Major Generals of the Divisions from which the detachment was ordered stating the number of deficiencies, and the companies, regiments and brigades from which they were severally detached; and on receipt of such notice the Major Generals will proceed by detail and draft and make up the deficiency from the proper companies, regiments and brigades, with the least possible delay, and cause them to rendezvous at such time and place as the officer commanding the detachment shall specify in his notice to the Major Generals. The commanding officer of the detachment will also cause suitable officers of his command to appear at the place of rendezvous appointed by him. And when the remaining part of his troops shall have assembled, they will proceed under the command of the senior officer thereof, to join the detachment. In all cases of making a draft, each Major General will cause returns thereof, both officers and men to be made to him, stating the companies, regiments and brigades from which they were severally taken. And in case any draft is made of troops and called into active service, Major Generals will in all cases cause the company officers, non-commissioned officers and privates to be immediately organized into companies, and forthwith returned as such to the office of the Adjutant General, and also to the commanding officer of the detachment at the time and place of rendezvous.

By the Commander-in-Chief.

A. B. THOMPSON,
Adj. Genl.

STATE OF MAINE.

HEADQUARTERS,
AUGUSTA, March 1, 1839.

General Order, No. 17.

Major General Charles W. Bodfish of the Eighth Division, will immediately order into the service of the State from his Division in addition to the detachment directed by General Order, No. 12, of February 27, 1839, four Captains, four Lieutenants, four Ensigns, sixteen Sergeants, four Drummers, four Fifers, and two hundred and fifty-six privates of Infantry; and one Captain, one Lieutenant, one Ensign, four Sergeants, one Drummer, one Fifer, and sixty-four privates of Light Infantry.

This additional draft will be armed, provided for in every respect, and rendezvous, as mentioned in General Order, No. 12, for the detachment in the Eighth Division, and remain in service three months, unless sooner discharged by the Commander-in-Chief.

By the Commander-in-Chief.

A. B. THOMPSON,
Adjutant General.

STATE OF MAINE.

HEADQUARTERS,
AUGUSTA, March 2, 1839.

General Order, No. 20.

Brigadier General John Williams, commanding officer of the third Division, will call out such force as may be necessary to fill up the detachment of one thousand men ordered from the third Division, February 16, 1839, on requisition of Major General Hodsdon stating the amount of the deficiency; and he will cause them to assemble at Bangor at such time, placed under command of such officer, and to march to such point, as Major General Hodsdon may direct. The commanding officer of the detachment to be ordered into service, will make requisition on Colonel George W. Stanley, Assistant Quartermaster at Bangor, for the necessary supplies for this march to join General Hodsdon's command.

By the Commander-in-Chief.

A. B. THOMPSON,
Adj: Genl.

STATE OF MAINE.

HEADQUARTERS,
AUGUSTA, March 8, 1839.

General Order, No. 23.

General Orders, Nos. 12 and 17, of February 27th and March 1st, 1839, so far as they relate to the troops in the Eighth Division, are countermanded as to the time appointed for the detachment to rendezvous. The officers and men of the detachment ordered into service by the before mentioned General Orders, will hold themselves in readiness to march at one hour's notice, to such place as may be required by the Commander-in-Chief.

Major General Bodfish will see the importance of promulgating this order with the least possible delay.
By the Commander-in-Chief.

A. B. THOMPSON,
Adj. Genl.

STATE OF MAINE.
HEADQUARTERS,
AUGUSTA, March 11, 1839.

General Order, No. 25.

The Commander-in-Chief directs the following as the component parts of the ration to be issued to the Militia of this State, when in actual service, viz.:—three-quarters of a pound of pork or bacon, or one and a quarter pounds of fresh or salt beef, eighteen ounces of bread or flour, or twelve ounces of hard bread, or one and a quarter pounds of corn meal, and at the rate of four pounds of soap, one and a half pounds of candles, two quarts of salt, four quarts of vinegar, eight quarts of peas or beans, and when practicable, two pounds of tea, and twelve pounds of sugar or the equivalent in molasses, to every one hundred rations.

No allowance will be made to troops who do not receive all the parts mentioned for the rations, but commissaries are directed to cause such parts thereof as can be furnished without great inconvenience and increased expense, to be delivered to the troops at every post when so required.

Officers commanding detachments in service will cause this order to be immediately promulgated that there may be no misapprehensions by any one in relation to the rations.

By the Commander-in-Chief.
(Signed)

A. B. THOMPSON,
Adjutant General.

STATE OF MAINE.
HEADQUARTERS,
AUGUSTA, March 25, 1839.

General Order, No. 28.

The detachment of troops from the Fifth and Sixth Divisions, now in the service of the State, under command of Colonel Orison Ripley, and at present stationed at Augusta, will be inspected, mustered and discharged, as follows, viz:

The Companies of Light Infantry and Riflemen from the Fifth Division, on Tuesday, the 26th; the Companies of Artillery, Light Infantry and Riflemen from the Sixth Division, on Wednesday the 27th; the A, B, C and D Companies of Infantry, on Thursday, the 28th; and the E, F, G and H Companies of Infantry, together with the field and staff officers, on Friday, the twenty-ninth days of March, instant.

Major General White, of the Second Division, is charged with the duty of inspecting and mustering the detachment aforesaid, and he will make immediate report thereof to the Adjutant General.

The detachment will be paid by companies at the office of the Adjutant General, immediately after the respective musters.

In directing the discharge of the troops under command of Colonel Ripley, the Commander-in-Chief avails himself of the occasion, to express to the detachment his warm thanks for the prompt manner in which they have responded to the call made for their services, as well as for their good conduct while quartered at the Capital. The rapid progress made in discipline, during the short time they have been on duty, is highly creditable to both officers and men, and it is another evidence that our patriotic citizen soldiery, while they are at all times ready to march in defence of our country's rights, also possess those qualities indispensable to the establishment of an efficient army "good order and subordination."

But in deciding that the condition of our border difficulties has so changed since the order directing the draft of militia from the Fifth and Sixth Divisions, as to render the services of this detachment not at present necessary, the Commander-in-Chief would remind them, that while he flatters himself with the hope that such justice will be done the State in regard to our boundary, as will render it unnecessary again to call in the aid of military power to preserve the integrity of our soil, yet that it is the duty of every community to be prepared to protect by physical force, those rights ever dear to a free people; and although the members of the detachment will forthwith return to their respective homes and firesides, they will recollect that their services may again be necessary; and should that emergency unfortunately occur, the Commander-in-Chief doubts not that they will respond to any further call, with that alacrity which has ever characterized the Militia of Maine.

By the Commander-in-Chief.
(Signed) A. B. THOMPSON,
Adjutant General.

STATE OF MAINE.

HEADQUARTERS,
AUGUSTA, March 25, 1839.

General Order, No. 29.

Major General Isaac Hodsdon, commanding the military force of the State now on duty on the northeastern frontier, will make immediate preparation for retiring with the troops of his command from the valley of the Aroostook; and as soon as a suitable civil force shall have been furnished the Land Agent, to enable that officer to protect the timber and other public property of which due notice will be given, he will cause the detachments under his orders to return by way of Houlton and the Aroostook road, to the city of Bangor.

By the Commander-in-Chief.
(Signed) A. B. THOMPSON,
Adj. Genl.

STATE OF MAINE.

HEADQUARTERS,
AUGUSTA, March 30, 1839.

General Order, No. 30.

Major General Isaac Hodsdon, commanding the State troops in actual service on the northeastern frontier, will leave of the detachment from the third Division, one Company of Light Infantry, one Company of Riflemen and two Companies of Infantry under command of a field officer, at Fort Fairfield and at the mouth of the Presque Isle of the Aroostook, for the purpose of protecting the public property, until a sufficient civil force is procured by the Land Agent for the object. General Hodsdon will forthwith return with the remaining portion of the detachment from the third Division, to the city of Bangor and he will report his command by Companies or larger divisions, as they arrive, to the Adjutant General at that place.

The detachment from the second Division, will without delay return to Bangor under Brigadier General Bachelder, who will report his command as the several Companies thereof shall arrive, to the Adjutant General at that city.

The officer left in command at Fort Fairfield and at the Presque Isle, on being notified by the Land Agent that a sufficient civil force has been procured to enable him to protect the public property, will immediately retire to Bangor with his command, and report to the Adjutant General.

Brigadier General Bachelder will leave a guard at township number ten on the Aroostook road, sufficient to protect such public stores as may from necessity be left at that post. This guard will be subject to the orders of the acting Quartermaster General.

Deeming it unnecessary longer to continue a military force on the northeastern frontier, the Commander-in-Chief directs that the Militia be discharged without delay; and he takes this occasion to express to the detachments from the second and third Divisions, his entire satisfaction with the manner in which they obeyed the call into the service of the State for the protection of the rights and honor of Maine; and their general conduct while in the public service, as reported by their respective commanding officers, merits, as it receives, his warm approbation.

Called into active service at a season unusual for military operations, without preparation and without experience, much inconvenience if not suffering must have been felt by the detachments on duty. It has been the intention of the Commander-in-Chief to render their condition one of as much comfort as the nature of the service would permit; and the zeal and alacrity with which they have obeyed the call for their aid, is sure evidence that Maine can rely with perfect confidence on the patriotism of her citizen soldiery, for the protection of her honor, and the vindication of her rights.

By the Commander-in-Chief.
(Signed) A. B. THOMPSON,
Adj. Gen.

STATE OF MAINE.
HEADQUARTERS,
AUGUSTA, April 4, 1839.
General Order, No. 31.

The detachment of troops from the Seventh Division, now in the service of the State under command of Major General Ezekiel Foster, and stationed at Calais, will be inspected, mustered, and discharged on Friday the fifth day of April, instant.

General Foster will make immediate report of the mustering of his detachment, to the Adjutant General in Calais.

The detachment will be paid by Companies at the quarters of the Adjutant General, immediately after they shall have been mustered.

The troops from the Seventh Division, having faithfully performed the service required of them, will now return to their several homes, from which they were unexpectedly called to protect the honor and defend the soil of Maine. The uniform good conduct of this detachment, as represented by its commanding officer, reflects high honor on both officers and men, and is evidence of that feeling of patriotism which inspires the hearts of those only who would be free.

Should the State require the further services of this Division, the Commander-in-Chief cannot doubt, that when called they will again rally round the standard of their country, in defence of those sacred rights purchased by the blood of our fathers.

By the Commander-in-Chief.
(Signed)   A. B. THOMPSON,
Adj. Genl.

STATE OF MAINE.
HEADQUARTERS,
AUGUSTA, April 8, 1839.
General Order, No. 31 1-2.

Major James Smith, commanding the troops stationed at Fort Fairfield and at the Presque Isle, will order the two companies of Infantry under his command to return to Bangor without delay. Major Smith will cause suitable provision to be made for subsistence and transportation on the march. The officers commanding the companies will report themselves to the Adjutant General at Bangor, on their arrival.

By the Commander-in-Chief.
(Signed)   A. B. THOMPSON,
Adj. Genl.

STATE OF MAINE.
HEADQUARTERS,
AUGUSTA, April 12, 1839.
General Order, No. 32.

The detachment of troops from the Second Division, now in active service under command of Brigadier General George W. Bachelder, will be inspected and mustered as follows, viz:

The "A" Company of Artillery, at present under command of Lieutenant Bates, and the Company of Infantry commanded by Captain Crane, on Saturday the thirteenth day of April instant, and the remaining part on the arrival of the several Companies at Bangor, and as will be designated by subsequent orders.

Brigadier General Bachelder will make immediate report of the mustering of his Companies, to the Adjutant General at Bangor.

The detachment will be paid by Companies at the quarters of the Adjutant General, immediately after they shall have been mustered.

Commanding officers will, without unnecessary delay, march their respective Companies to Augusta, where, upon their arrival, they will forthwith discharge their men.

All officers will consider themselves relieved from active service, on the discharge of their respective commands.

By the Commander-in-Chief.
(Signed)   A. B. THOMPSON,
Adj. Genl.

STATE OF MAINE.
HEADQUARTERS,
AUGUSTA, April 12, 1839.

General Order, No. 33.

The detachment of troops in actual service under command of Brigadier General George W. Bachelder, will, on the arrival of the Companies in to the City of Bangor, occupy such quarters as may be furnished by Assistant Quarter Master George W. Stanley.

By the Commander-in-Chief.
(Signed)   A. B. THOMPSON,
Adjutant General.

STATE OF MAINE.
HEADQUARTERS,
AUGUSTA, April 15, 1839.

General Order, No. 34.

The Company of Cavalry in the service of the State from the Third Division, under command of Captain Smart, and now quartered in Bangor, will be inspected, mustered and discharged on Tuesday, the sixteenth day of April, instant.

Major General Hodsdon will make immediate report of the inspection and mustering of the Cavalry, to the Adjutant General at Bangor.

The Company of Cavalry will be paid at the quarters of the Adjutant General at Bangor, immediately after it shall have been mustered.

By the Commander-in-Chief.
(Signed)   A. B. THOMPSON,
Adj. Genl.

AROOSTOOK WAR.

TIME OF OFFICERS

Names.	Rank.	Period of Service. From	Period of Service. To	Place of residence.
Isaac Hodsdon	Major General	17 Feb. 1839	26 Apr. 1839	Bangor...
Ezekiel Foster	Major General	25 Feb. 1839	5 Apr. 1839	Pembroke
Joseph C. Stevens	Division Inspector..	13 Mar.1839 / 11 May 1839	30 Apr. 1839 / 13 May 1839	Bangor.
Joseph N. Prescott	Division Inspector	24 Feb. 1839	5 Apr. 1839	Calais.....
John L. Hodsdon	Aid to Major General..	20 Feb. 1839	25 Apr. 1839	Exeter....
Oliver Frost	Aid to Major General..	20 Feb. 1839	26 Apr. 1839	Bangor...
William H. McCrillis	Aid to Major General..	20 Feb. 1839	15 Mar.1839	Bangor...
Aaron Hayden, Jr	Aid to Major General..	25 Feb. 1839	5 Apr. 1839	Eastport..
Joseph Gilman	Division Q. M	20 Feb. 1839	25 Apr. 1839	Dixmont.
Henry Warren	Asst. Division Q. M	18 Feb. 1839	25 Apr. 1839	Bangor...
Ebenezer G. Rawson	Asst. Division Q. M	20 Feb. 1839	25 Apr. 1839	Bangor..
Paul Varney	Asst. Division Q. M	21 Feb. 1839	25 Apr. 1839	
Daniel Wood	Asst. Division Q. M	21 Feb. 1839	25 Apr. 1839	Bangor...
Henry E. Prentiss	Capt. of Engineers	20 Feb. 1839	20 Apr. 1839	Bangor...
Elijah L. Hamlin	Sup. of Vidette	20 Feb. 1839	25 Apr. 1839	Bangor...
Samuel Smith	Asst. Sup. of Vidette..	23 Feb. 1839	15 Apr. 1839	Bangor...
John Sargent, Jr	Forage Master	26 Feb. 1839	25 Apr. 1839	Bangor...
George W. Batchelder	Brigadier General	22 Feb. 1839	23 Apr. 1839	Gardiner.
George S. Carpenter	Brigadier Major....	25 Feb. 1839 / 29 Mar.1839	27 Feb. 1839 / 19 Apr. 1839	Augusta
Salon S. Simons	Act. Brigadier Major..	27 Feb. 1839	29 Mar.1839	Fairfield..
Joshua Carpenter	Act. Brigadier Major..	1 Mar. 1839	24 Apr. 1839	Lincoln or Bangor?..
David C. B. Bowman	Aid to Brig. General..	25 Feb. 1839	19 Apr. 1839	Gardiner.
Henry Morrill	Brigadier Q. M	25 Feb. 1839	19 Apr. 1839	Augusta..
John Philbrick	Colonel	25 Feb. 1839	19 Apr. 1839	Mt.Vernon
Orison Ripley	Colonel	4 Mar. 1839	29 Mar.1839	Paris.....
David Walker	Colonel	20 Feb. 1839	25 Apr. 1839	
Isaac N. Tucker	Lieutenant Colonel	25 Feb. 1839	19 Apr. 1839	
Charles Andrews	Lieutenant Colonel	6 Mar. 1839	29 Mar.1839	Turner-..
Lysander Cutler	Lieutenant Colonel	20 Feb. 1839	25 Apr. 1839	Dexter....
George W. Cummings	Lieutenant Colonel	20 Feb. 1839	25 Apr. 1839	Bangor...
Moses H. Young	Lieutenant Colonel	20 Feb. 1839	5 Mar. 1839	
Samuel Wood, Jr	Major	25 Feb. 1839	19 Apr. 1839	Winthrop.
Nathaniel Norcross	Major	6 Mar. 1839	29 Mar.1839	
William Tarbox	Adjutant	25 Feb. 1839	19 Apr. 1839	Gardiner.
Joseph Barrows	Adjutant	6 Mar. 1839	29 Mar.1839	
Charles Palmer	Adjutant	20 Feb. 1839	25 Apr. 1839	Belfast...
Foxwell C. Marr	Quartermaster	25 Feb. 1839	19 Apr. 1839	
Orvill Knight	Quartermaster	6 Mar. 1839	29 Mar.1839	
Daniel T. Jewett	Quartermaster	20 Feb. 1839	25 Apr. 1839	Bangor...
Albert G. Bodfish	Paymaster	25 Feb. 1839	18 Apr. 1839	
Benjamin P. Swan	Paymaster	6 Mar. 1839	29 Mar.1839	
Charles Blanchard	Chaplain	25 Feb. 1839	19 Apr. 1839	
George Bates	Chaplain	6 Mar. 1839	29 Mar.1839	
Joseph C. Lovejoy	Chaplain	23 Feb. 1839	25 Apr. 1839	Orono..
Robert A. Cony	Surgeon	25 Feb. 1839	19 Apr. 1839	Augusta..
John Grover	Surgeon	6 Mar. 1839	3 Apr. 1839	
Paul Ruggles	Surgeon	23 Feb. 1839	13 May 1839	Carmel...
Charles C. Porter	Surgeon	7 Mar. 1839	5 Apr. 1839	Calais.....
Moses Frost	Surgeon's Mate	25 Feb. 1839	19 Apr. 1839	
Jesse P. Sweat	Surgeon's Mate	6 Mar. 1839	29 Mar.1839	
Lewis Watson	Surgeon's Mate	20 Feb. 1839	25 Apr. 1839	Bangor...

AROOSTOOK WAR. 23

IN SERVICE AT AROOSTOOK.

Place of rendezvous.	Place of discharge.	No. of miles to place of rendezvous and from place of discharge.	Subsistence—No. of rations.	Forage—No. of rations.	No. of servants actually kept in service.	No. of horses actually kept in service.	Remarks.
Bangor	Bangor		200		4	7	
Calais	Calais	80		*	2	2	*Received forage in kind.
Bangor	Bangor					2	3 Entitled to additional rations for extra service and commanding separate post 9 days.
Calais	Calais				1		
Bangor	Bangor	50			2	3	Entitled to additional allowance as Division Inspector, twenty-four days.
Bangor	Bangor				2	3	
Bangor	Houlton	120			2	3	
Calais	Calais	60			2	1	
Bangor	Bangor	50			2	3	
Bangor	Bangor				1	1	
Bangor	Bangor				1	1	
Bangor	Bangor			45	1	1	
Bangor	Bangor				1	1	
Bangor	Bangor				1	3	
Bangor	Bangor						
Bangor	Bungor						
Bangor	Bangor			*			*Received forage in kind, 1 mo.
Augusta	Augusta	15	40	21	3	5	
Augusta	Augusta	70	20	10½	2	3	
Augusta		230	20	10½	2	3	
Houlton	Bangor	120			2	3	
Augusta	Bangor	80	40	21	1	2	
Augusta	Bangor	70	40	21	1	2	
Augusta	Bangor	105	16		1	3	Entitled to additional rations as commander of a post 9 days.
Augusta	Augusta	100			2	2	
Bangor	Bangor	100	30	15	2	4	
Augusta	Bangor	85			1	2	
Augusta	Augusta	80			2	3	
Bangor	Bangor	80	10	16	2	3	Entitled to additional rations as commander of a post, 4 days.
Bangor	Bangor					2	3 Entitled to additional rations as commander of a post 23 days.
Bangor		180			2	2	
Augusta	Bangor	95			2	2	Entitled to additional rations as commander of a post 30 days.
Augusta	Augusta	70			2	3	
Augusta	Bangor	85	34	21	2	1	
Augusta	Augusta	100			1	2	
Bangor	Bangor	70		15	1	2	
Augusta	Bangor	90	42		1		
Augusta	Augusta	90			1		
Bangor	Bangor		34	10½	1	2	
Augusta	Bangor	95			1		
Augusta	Augusta	140			1		
Augusta	Bangor	70	14	43	1	3	
Augusta	Augusta	80			1		
Bangor	Bangor	25	270	6	2	3	
Augusta	Bangor	70			2	3	
Augusta	Augusta	140			1	1	Extra R. for length of service.
Bangor	Bangor	30	49	18	2	4	
Calais	Calais				1	2	
Augusta	Bangor	90	42		1	2	
Augusta	Augusta	200			1	1	
Bangor	Bangor		12		1	2	

TIME OF OFFICERS

Names.	Rank.	Period of Service. From	To	Place of residence.
Henry Smith	Sergeant Major	25 Feb. 1839	19 Apr. 1839	
Cyrus Wormell	Sergeant Major	6 Mar.1839	12 Mar.1839	
William P. Frost	Sergeant Major	12 Mar.1839	29 Mar.1839	
Charles Barnard	Sergeant Major	20 Feb. 1839	5 Mar.1839	
George Noyes	Sergeant Major	6 Mar.1839	25 Apr. 1839	
Nathaniel P. Page	Q. M. Sergeant	25 Feb. 1839	18 Apr. 1839	
Warren I. Remick	Q. M. Sergeant	6 Mar.1839	29 Mar.1839	
Lemuel Ellis	Prin. Musician	20 Feb. 1839	23 Apr. 1839	
William A. Herrick	Drum Major	25 Feb. 1839	19 Apr. 1839	
Edmund Irish, Jr	Drum Major	6 Mar.1839	29 Mar.1839	
John M. Shaw	Drum Major	25 Mar.1839	23 Apr. 1839	
Samuel Q. Bean	Fife Major	25 Feb. 1839	18 Apr. 1839	
Daniel Delano	Fife Major	8 Mar.1839	29 Mar.1839	
Jerome Nichols	Fife Major	2 Mar.1839	25 Apr. 1839	
John Fairbanks	Major of Artillery	25 Feb. 1839	18 Apr. 1839	Winthrop
James Smith	Major of Artillery	20 Feb. 1839	30 Apr. 1839	
Amos Pickard	{ Lieutenant	20 Feb. 1839	5 Apr. 1839	} Ham'd'n
	⎰ Adjt. of Artillery	6 Apr.1839	13 May 1839	
Samuel D. Erskine	Q. M. of Artillery	6 Mar.1839	29 Mar.1839	
Samuel P. Leighton	Q. M. of Artillery	1 Mar.1839	30 Apr. 1839	Bangor
Enoch Perkins	Paymaster of Artillery	7 Mar.1839	13 Mar.1839	
James R. Hanley	Paymaster of Artillery	13 Mar.1839	29 Mar.1839	

Supernumerary

Names.	Rank.	From	To	Place of residence.
Benjamin Stockin	Captain	25 Feb. 1839	26 Feb. 1839	
Joseph S. Bishop	Captain	25 Feb. 1839	7 Mar.1839	Wayne
Phineas Howe	Captain	6 Mar.1839	9 Mar.1839	
James Walker	Captain	6 Mar.1839	9 Mar.1839	Lovell
Eliphalet Miller	Captain	20 Feb. 1839	26 Apr. 1839	
David Dow	Captain	20 Feb. 1839	24 Apr. 1839	
Truxton Dougherty	Captain	20 Feb. 1839	2 Mar.1839	
Gustavus Clark	Lieutenant	25 Feb. 1839	8 Mar.1839	
Elden Barker	Lieutenant	6 Mar.1839	7 Mar.1839	Lovell
Jabez Bradbury	Lieutenant	20 Feb. 1839	11 Mar.1839	
James B. Cleaveland	Lieutenant	20 Feb.1839	4 Mar.1839	
Thomas Wright	Ensign	6 Mar.1839	8 Mar.1839	
Jacob P. Saunders	Ensign	20 Feb. 1839	23 Apr. 1839	
Jeremiah Lord	Ensign	20 Feb. 1839	25 Apr. 1839	
Haskell W. Johnson	Ensign	20 Feb. 1839	24 Apr. 1839	

AROOSTOOK WAR. 25

IN SERVICE AT AROOSTOOK—Concluded.

Place of rendezvous.	Place of discharge.	No. of miles to place of rendezvous and from place of discharge.	Subsistence and Forage received in kind.		No. of servants actually kept in service.	No. of horses actually kept in service.	Remarks.
			Subsistence—No. of rations.	Forage—No. of rations.			
Augusta..	Bangor...	85	16				
Augusta..	Augusta..	90					
Augusta..	Augusta..						
Bangor...	Houlton..	160					
Bangor...	Bangor...	20					
Augusta..	Bangor...	90					
Augusta..	Augusta..	180					
Bangor...	Bangor...	80					
Augusta..	Bangor...	40					
Augusta..	Augusta..	70					
Bangor...	Bangor...	35					
Augusta..	Bangor..	30					
Augusta..	Augusta..	90					
Bangor...	Bangor...	30					
Augusta..	Augusta..	25	63		2	3	
Bangor...	Ft.Fairf'ld	180	68	75	2	3	Entitled to additional rations for commanding a separate post 24 days.
Bangor...	Bangor...	20	60		1	2	Appointed Adjt. to Bat. and Maj. Smith after troops were recalled, 2 C. being left.
Augusta..	Augusta..	80			1		
....	....	180	91		1		
Augusta..	Augusta..						
Augusta..	Augusta..	110			1		

Officers.

Augusta..	Augusta..	30			1		Que.
Augusta..	....	110					
Augusta..	Augusta..	70	4				
Augusta..	Augusta..	160			1		
Bangor...	Bangor...	70	42		1		
Bangor...	Bangor...	50	46		1		
Bangor...	....	150			1		
Augusta..	....	30					
Augusta..	Augusta..	160			1		
Bangor...	....	105	5		1		
Bangor...							
Augusta..	Augusta..	75					
Bangor...	Bangor...	50	51		1		
Bangor...	Bangor...	100	47		1		
Bangor...	Bangor...	75	60		1		

Muster Roll of Captain Joseph Anthony's Company of Infantry in the Detachment of drafted Militia of Maine, called into actual service by the State, for the protection of its Northeastern Frontier, from the twenty-fifth day of February, 1839, the time of its rendezvous at Augusta, Maine, to the nineteenth day of April, 1839, when mustered.

CAPTAIN.	LIEUTENANT.	ENSIGN.
Joseph Anthony.	....	Charles Simmons.
SERGEANTS.	CORPORALS.	MUSICIANS.
Horace S. Cooley.	Charles Hamlin.	Harrison Stone.
Simon Pratt.	Henry L. Carter.	James Trask.
Epaphrus R. Bryant.	Micah Safford.	
S. S. Webster.	E. E. Dennis.	
William H. Clark.		
Thomas Field.		
	PRIVATES.	
Blake, Dudley.	Heath, John.	Robey, John, Jr.
Bodwell, David.	Herrin, Samuel.	Rollins, Joseph.
Briggs, John.	Knowles, Harrison.	Saben, John.
Cogan, William E. D.	Lamson, John.	Savage, Daniel, 2d.
Fletcher, Joseph H.	Lyon, David.	Trask, Samuel.
Gazlin, Benjamin.	Lyon, Ezra.	Wells, Lewis.
Gilley, Isaac F.	Morgan, Theophilus.	Wiggins, Ephraim.
Godfrey, Adam.	Packard, Sidney.	Wilson, Jesse.
Greene, Sumner.	Partridge, John.	Wright, John.
Guild, Samuel.	Place, William.	Young, John.
Haskell, Greenleaf.	Pray, Edmund, Jr.	

Muster Roll of Captain Albion P. Arnold's Company of Artillery in the Detachment of drafted Militia of Maine, called into actual service by the State, for the protection of its Northeastern Frontier, from the twenty-fifth day of February, 1839, the time of its rendezvous at Augusta, Maine, to the seventeenth day of April, 1839, when discharged or mustered.

CAPTAIN.
Albion P. Arnold.

LIEUTENANT.
Charles B. Bates.

ENSIGN.
....

SERGEANTS.
George W. Armstrong.
Sylvanus Fairbanks.
Rufus K. Lane.
John S. Morrill.

CORPORALS.
Daniel F. Ayer.
William P. Caldwell.
Cyrus C. Fairbanks.
William Walker.

MUSICIANS.
Charles E. Hodges.
Sumner Smith.

PRIVATES.

Allen, George.
Allen, Josiah.
Atwood, George M.
Blaisdell, Orrin W.
Brown, John W.
Butler, Samuel.
Campbell, Rufus.
Choate, James R.
Dudley, Stephen.
Earle, Joseph.
Fogg, Francis A.
Follett, John E.
Folsom, Cyrus H.

Haines, George W.
Hall, Samuel P.
Hammond, George W.
Jacobs, John.
Knowles, Augustus.
Knowles, John.
Lawton, Daniel.
Leeman, Moses D.
Lyon, William.
Melvin, Adorno L.
Moody, Edlon D.
Moshier, Stephen.
Page, Charles R.

Page, David L.
Patch, Jonathan.
Perkins, William.
Pinkham, William.
Quint, Ivory.
Ramsdell, Harvey.
Russell, Samuel B.
Stanley, George W.
Webster, Nathan.
Whittier, Jonathan.
Wiggin, James M.
Yeaton, Phineas, Jr.

Muster Roll of Captain Benjamin Beals' Company of Infantry in the Detachment of drafted Militia of Maine, called into actual service by the State, for the protection of its Northeastern Frontier, from the twenty-fifth day of February, 1839, the time of its rendezvous at Augusta, Maine, to the seventeenth day of April, 1839, when mustered.

CAPTAIN.
Benjamin Beals.

LIEUTENANT.
Lora B. Stevens.

ENSIGN.
Daniel Foss.

SERGEANTS.
George Gould.
John E. Sawyer.
David Wheeler.
Elias L. Lothrop.

CORPORALS.
Harrison Rose.
Loren Parcher.
Gustavus Gilbert.
William Day.

MUSICIANS.
George Austin.
Leonard Griffin.

Additon, Charles A.
Bishop, Zadoc.
Carver, Caleb.
Caswell, Chandler.
Caswell, Marcus.
Clark, Amos, Jr.
Coffin, James, Jr.
Cummings, Jesse A.
Day, Samuel B.

PRIVATES.
Dunn, David T.
Foss, Levi.
George, George W.
Gilbert, John N.
Gilbert, Judson.
Grover, John.
Gould, Joseph.
Harvey, Harrison.
Hodgdon, Ebenezer.

Mitchell, Jesse.
Palmer, Manley.
Pettengill, Jason.
Ricker, Harris.
Sedgely, Edward.
Stetson, Benjamin F.
Stetson, Nathaniel.
Stubbs, Lorenzo D.
Thoms, Peter A.

AROOSTOOK WAR.

Muster Roll of Captain Henry Bailey's Company of Infantry in the Detachment of drafted Militia of Maine, called into actual service by the State, for the protection of its Northeastern Frontier from the fifth day of March, 1839, the time of its rendezvous at Calais, Maine, to the sixth day of April, 1839, when discharged or mustered.

CAPTAIN.
Henry Bailey.

LIEUTENANT.
John A. Brown.

ENSIGN.
William Worster.

SERGEANTS.
Pickering Patten.
Zenas Wheeler.
Curtis Merritt.
John Church.

CORPORALS.
Moses Worster, Jr.
Joshua W. Norton.
Nathan G. Peasley.
Amos Whitten.

MUSICIANS.
Archibald Smith.
James P. Lawrence.

PRIVATES.

Allen, Joseph S.
Bagley, James.
Beal, William D.
Caler, John B.
Caligan, Humphrey.
Chandler, Barnabas S.
Church, George W.
Connery, John.
Cotton, William.
Crowley, Nathaniel.
Cummings, Amos.
Cummings, Samuel B.
Cummings, William B.
Dorr, John F.
Dorr, Joseph P.
Dorr, Leonard W.
Dorr, Moses W.
Dorr, Richard B.
Farr, James.
Farnsworth, George.

Foster, William.
Grant, Ephraim.
Grant, James D.
Holmes, William.
Jacques, William.
Knowlton, Joel.
Leighton, James.
Low, Lehi.
McCarthy, Charles.
McCaslin, Amaziah N.
McCaslin, Stephen J.
McKinsey, Joseph D.
McLure, James.
Newingham, Nicholas.
O'Brien, Matthew.
Peabody, Joshua.
Pickett, James.
Plummer, Fellars.
Reynolds, James.
Richardson, Enoch.

Sinclair, William.
Skinner, Justin.
Small, Elbridge G. W.
Smith, Moses.
Smith, Russell.
Steward, Temple C.
Tabberts, Jeremiah.
Tabberts, John 2d.
Tabberts, Otis.
Tabberts, Samuel H.
Tinney, Otis.
Tucker, John.
Turner, Patrick.
Whitney, Asa B.
Willey, Amos P.
Woodward, Thomas.
Worster, Isaac Jr.
Worster, John Jr.
Worster, Mark.
Wright, Thomas.

Muster Roll of Captain Nathan Barker's Company of Light Infantry in the Detachment of drafted Militia of Maine, called into actual service by the State, for the protection of its Northeastern Frontier, from the sixth day of March, 1839, the time of its rendezvous at Augusta, Maine, to the twenty-sixth day of March, 1839, when discharged or mustered.

CAPTAIN.	LIEUTENANT.	ENSIGN.
Nathan Barker.	Ephriam Harmon.	John S. Willson.
SERGEANTS.	CORPORALS.	MUSICIANS.
Simon A. Dyer.	James W. Stevens.	Thomas Pennell.
Benjamin Boothby.	Stephen Swett.	William Pike.
Lothrop Worcester.	S. V. R. G. Brown.	
William Proctor.	Henry Towle.	

PRIVATES.

Babb, Joseph H.	Fernald, Samuel R.	Morris, William E.
Bacon, Samuel F.	Field, Amos, Jr.	Newcomb, Lowell.
Bailey, John H.	Frye, John.	Paine, Brian.
Bangs, Samuel S.	Garland, John.	Patterson, James.
Barbour, Seward P.	Gower, Henry E.	Pike, George W.
Bean, George T.	Green, Charles M.	Purinton, Joseph C.
Bond, John.	Hale, Joseph W.	Richards, Francis.
Bragdon, Nathaniel.	Harmon, Albert.	Rolf, David F.
Bragdon, Seth L.	Harris, George.	Rounds, George.
Buckman, Samuel.	Hasty, James M.	Sands, Isaac.
Bullard, Asa.	Haynes, James M.	Sawyer, Ethan A.
Chandler, Charles F.	Hutchinson, Mark.	Sawyer, Francis O.
Clark, John M.	Leathers, William W.	Shaw, Nelson.
Coffin, Isiah.	Libby, Benjamin F.	Smith, Amos.
*Davice, John C.	Longley, David M.	Strout, David P.
Donnell, Francis.	Mead, Jason.	Swett, Alfred.
Dyer, Alfred.	Merrill, Curtis B.	Tuckerman, John.
Dyer, George W.	Merrill, Daniel.	Winslow, Oliver.
Duran, Benjamin.	Merrill, John.	Whitten, Joseph.
Emery, Joshua T.	Merrill, Rufus N.	Whitney, Levi, Jr.

*On pay roll as John C. Davis.

AROOSTOOK WAR. 31

Muster Roll of Captain John D. Barnard's Company of Infantry in the Detachment of drafted Militia of Maine, called into actual service by the State, for the protection of its Northeastern Frontier, from the sixth day of March, 1839, the time of its rendezvous at Augusta, Maine, to the twenty-eighth day of March, 1839, when discharged or mustered.

CAPTAIN.
John D. Barnard.

LIEUTENANT.
David R. Gleason.

ENSIGN.
Samuel Bird.

SERGEANTS.
John N. Thompson.
Daniel G. Holt.
Ephraim K. Andrews.
Alpheus W. Strickland.

CORPORALS.
George W. Taylor.
William Bartlett.
William Walker.
Samuel Marston.

MUSICIANS.

PRIVATES.

Abbot, Aaron J.
Akers, William J.
Austin, Hezekiah.
Barbrick, Moses.
Barker, Joseph.
Barker, Waterman.
Bean, George.
Bean, Josiah.
Bean, Vear.
Beattie, Patterson.
Bennett, Gilman.
Besse, Joshua.
Booker, Washington.
Brown, John.
Brown, Joseph.
Chase, Dudley.

Coffin, Jonathan C.
Coffin, Samuel F.
Edmands, Benjamin, Jr.
Elkins, Edward N.
Emery, Amos.
Garmon, Wilmath S., Jr.
Gilcrease, Hiram.
Glines, Daniel G.
Grover, Almon.
Heath, Joseph, Jr.
Holt, Abbot.
Judkins, Josiah A.
Kendal, Daniel G.
Kilgore, Moses H.
Libbey, Josiah.
Mills, Cyrus.

Mitchell, Franklin.
Morton, Daniel.
Newton, James N.
Simpson, Benjamin.
Simpson, Daniel F.
Simpson, John.
Simpson, Joseph.
Smith, Seth E.
Tripp, James S.
Walker, Jason H.
Williams, Bela.
Wight, Joseph R.
Young, James.
York, Ebenezer.
York, Isaac J.
York, Randall.

Muster Roll of Captain Samuel Burrell's Company of Infantry in the Detachment of drafted Militia of Maine, called into actual service by the State, for the protection of its Northeastern Frontier, from the twenty-fifth day of February, 1839, the time of its rendezvous at Augusta, Maine, to the nineteenth day of April, 1839, when discharged or mustered.

CAPTAIN.
Samuel Burrell.

LIEUTENANT.
John J. Emery.

ENSIGN.
Charles Cornforth.

SERGEANTS.
James Hasty, Jr.
Elias C. Hallet.
William Gardiner.
William L. Maxwell.

CORPORALS.
John Bradbury.
Ephraim O. Leach.
David W. Tinkham.
Thurston H. Tozier.

MUSICIANS.
Josiah Pearl.
Silas Richardson.

PRIVATES.

Banks, David P.
Bradbury, Reuben.
Branch, Adrastus.
Boston, Greshom.
Burleigh, Walter.
Church, Charles.
Clifford, Isaac B.
Corson, Benjamin F.
Corson, Eben S.
Davis, William.
Dillingham, Charles E.
Emery, Briggs H., 2d.
Evans, John.
Fogg, Joseph.
Gibbs, Heman, Jr.

Greene, William.
Hayward, James.
Healy, Moses, Jr.
Higgins, Abisha.
Holmes, James.
Johnson, Chancellor.
Lander, William.
McGrath, Theodore.
Peavey, Joseph.
Peavey, Joseph C.
Peavey, William.
Priest, George W.
Pullen, Granville D.
Ricker, Ivory.
Ricker, Joseph, Jr.

Rines, John.
Rose, George.
Shorey, Henry A.
Sibley, Peter, Jr.
Smith, Hartson.
Southwick, William.
Tobey, Curtis.
Tozier, William P.
Whitcomb, Sewall.
Whitcomb, Thomas.
Woodman, William.
Wyman, Charles
Wyman, James.
Wyman, James E.

AROOSTOOK WAR.

Muster Roll of Captain Hiram Burnham's Company of Light Infantry in the Detachment of drafted Militia of Maine, called into actual service by the State, for the protection of its Northeastern Frontier, from the third day of March, 1839, the time of its rendezvous at Calais, Maine, to the sixth day of April, 1839, when discharged or mustered.

CAPTAIN.
Hiram Burnham.

SERGEANTS.
Michael L. Patten.
John W. Coffin.
Ephraim Wille.
Thomas J. Smith.

Baker, Forbes.
Bracey, William.
Campbell, James M.
Campbell, Samuel.
Colson, Samuel, Jr.
Conners, John.
Curtis, Calvin B.
Dorman, Ephram P.
Dunbar, Alfred.
Dunbar, John B.
Dyer, Emery.
Everett, Charles H.
Freeman, George.
Giles, Ebenezer.

LIEUTENANT.
William B. Austin.

CORPORALS.
Robert F. Campbell.
Samuel Conners.
William H. Stevens.
John Rumble.

PRIVATES.
Godfrey, David.
Guptill, Lemuel.
Kellier, William.
Kelley, Francis.
Kilton, William.
Kincaid, Samuel.
Kingsley, Rufus.
Leighton, Seamen.
Lewis, Everett.
Madden, Rufus.
McRoy, Francis.
Parker, Henry D.
Parker, Luther.
Parret, Stilman.

ENSIGN.
Robert Moore.

MUSICIANS.
Ambrose Campbell.
James Campbell.

Patten, Francis B.
Preble, Galen O.
Shaw, John.
Sinclair, Benjamin.
Small, James 2d.
Smith, Andrew.
Springer, Leamon S.
Stevens, Luther.
Steward, George.
Strout, Horace.
White, Stillman S.
White, Thomas A.
Whitmore, John.
Whitney, Ephraim.
Wille, Andrew.
Wingate, George.

Muster Roll of Captain Daniel W. Clark's Company of Infantry, in the Detachment of drafted Militia of Maine, called into actual service by the State, for the protection of its Northeastern Frontier, from the sixth day of March, 1839, the time of its rendezvous at Calais, Maine, to the fifth day of April, 1839, when discharged or mustered.

CAPTAIN.
Daniel W. Clark.

LIEUTENANT.
Nathan A. Swan.

ENSIGN.
Moses McFarland.

SERGEANTS.
Samuel Scammons.
Asa Googins.
Benjamin Smith.
Ezra D. Reed.

CORPORALS.
Isaac Smith.
Philip Hodgkins.
Elbridge G. Uran.
Albert G. Berry.

MUSICIANS.
John S. Emery.
Samuel Springer.

Aldrich, Asa L.
Alley, Hiram.
Ashley, Frederic.
Bacon, Francis.
Bartlett, David.
Beane, William.
Brown, James.
Buckley, Franklin.
Bunker, Benjamin J.
Bunker, Sewall.
Butler Ambrose.
Butler Ansel.
Butler, Nathaniel R.
Clark, Ensign.
Clark, John M.
Colson, Jonas.
Coats, Thomas G.
Coolidge, Silas.
Day, Edmond.
Dyer, Asa.

PRIVATES.
Dyer, Joel.
Foss, Thomas.
Gilley, William.
Gilpatrick, Ignatius.
Gordon, Joseph M.
Gordon, Paul S.
Googins, Thomas.
Gott, James.
Hardison, Sabin.
Hardison, Stephen 2d.
Hastings, Richard.
Higgins, Adoniram.
Higgins, Nehemiah.
Howard Amos.
King, James 2d.
Lervey, Samuel, Jr.
Lopans, Abraham W.
Mayo, James.
Moor, Isaiah.
More, Eben P.

Morris, Benjamin.
Norris, George.
Norwood, Jonathan.
Norwood, Samuel.
Nutter, Lemuel.
Perry, David.
Richardson, Erastus H.
Richardson, Leander.
Richardson, Joseph.
Robinson, William.
Sawyer, Benjamin.
Scammons, Dudley.
Springer, William.
Springer, Samuel.
Wentworth, John.
Whitaker, Andrew.
Whitaker, Oren.
Williams, George.
Young, Winthrop.

AROOSTOOK WAR. 35

Muster Roll of Captain James Clark's Company of Light Infantry in the Detachment of drafted Militia of Maine, called into actual service by the State, for the protection of its Northeastern Frontier, from the twentieth day of February, 1839, the time of its rendezvous at Bangor, Maine, to the eleventh day of May, 1839, when discharged or mustered.

CAPTAIN.	LIEUTENANT.	ENSIGN.
James Clark.	William E. Atwood.	Nathaniel D. Eaton.
SERGEANTS.	CORPORALS.	MUSICIANS.
Joseph Leslie.	William M. Johnson.	John Swan.
Solomon York.	Ezekiel C. Jackson.	Jacob Swan.
John N. Emerson.	Laomi S. Herrick.	Amazias Dodge.
Timothy M. Cook.	Hazen Messenger.	
	PRIVATES.	
Allen, Samuel.	Grover, Abraham.	Reed, George B.
Baker, Edward D.	Hale, Reuben.	Reed, Harvey.
Baker, Samuel.	Harris, William.	Rose, Joseph.
Barden, Oren.	Herrin, Bowman.	Sargent, Darius.
Bean, Carlos.	Herrick, Thomas C.	Shaw, John.
Bither, Ira.	Hewes, Daniel.	Shaw, Nathan S.
Blake, Levi.	Hinckley, Lorenzo.	Smith, Gorham.
Blagdon, Samuel.	Howard, Charles A.	Spratt, Dudley D.
Budge, John N.	Jenness, John.	Stevens, Howard.
Bunker, Silas, Jr.	Low, Charles.	Stinchfield, Daniel L.
Chadman, John O.	Luce, Freeman.	Swan, Hiram.
Corliss, William.	Mansel, Ira.	Swan, Nathaniel.
Cross, William.	Mayo, Enoch R.	Sylvester, Elijah.
Cushman, Joseph.	Mayo, William H.	Triggs, Augustine.
Dunning, Valentine.	Mcintire, Philip.	Vincent, Willard.
Dyer, Benjamin.	Miller, Jason.	Wadleigh, Azariah.
Eddy, George W.	Millet, Samuel V.	Walker, Aaron H.
Foss, John E.	Mitchell, Nelson.	Webber, George B.
French, David.	Myrick, Reuben.	Wheelden, Peter.
Glidden, Hiram.	Norcross, Israel.	Whittier, Charles.
Goodwin, Francis.	Patterson,. Benjamin.	Willey, William.
Grant, Arthur L.	Perkins, Nathaniel.	
	Prescott, James.	

AROOSTOOK WAR.

Muster Roll of Captain Reuben Crane, 2d's, Company of Infantry in the Detachment of drafted Militia of Maine, called into actual service by the State, for the protection of its Northeastern Frontier, from the twenty-fifth day of February, 1839, the time of its rendezvous at Augusta, Maine, to the thirteenth day of April, 1839, when discharged or mustered.

CAPTAIN.	LIEUTENANT.	ENSIGN.
Reuben Crane, 2d.	Samuel B. Davis.	Wellington Hunton.
SERGEANTS.	CORPORALS.	MUSICIANS.
David Boynton, 2d.	Samuel Tuck, 2d.	Cyrus Brown.
David McGaffey, Jr.	John Stevens.	Samuel S. Gilman.
Jonathan E. Robinson.	Jacob Rundlett.	Matthias Smith.
Jesse G. Tuck.	Joseph Blake.	
Albert Storer.		
	PRIVATES.	
Batchelder, David, 2d.	Greene, Harrison B.	Philbrick, John R.
Bean, John H.	Griffin, Edward.	Philbrick, Oliver S.
Bishop, William H.	Haines, Howard.	Pool, Henry O.
Butler, Jarius.	Hill, Henry B.	Randall, Asa.
Chapman, Benjamin P.	House, James L.	Richardson, John, Jr.
Clough, George W.	Hutchins, Henry.	Richardson, Samuel H.
Cole, Sumner.	Jackman, William C.	Robinson, David.
Dane, Francis B.	Jones, George.	Sias, Moses P.
Dane, Solomon S.	Ladd, Reuben.	Smith, Charles.
Dudley, John S.	Leighton, Lemuel.	Smith, John.
Dudley, Moses S.	Leighton, Samuel, Jr.	Stain, John D.
Dudley, William K.	Lock, Josiah R.	Stevens, Samuel.
Dugan, Merrill.	Lord, William.	Tuck, Joseph, 2d.
Farrington, Samuel.	Morse, Samuel.	Watson, James H.
Fellows, Moses.	Moshier, Davis.	Woods, George W.
French, George.	Norris, Benjamin.	Woods, Sampson.
Gile, Samuel H.	Palmer, Thomas F.	

AROOSTOOK WAR. 37

Muster Roll of **Captain Daniel Dority's Company** of Infantry in the Detachment of drafted Militia of Maine, called into actual service by the State, for the protection of its Northeastern Frontier, from the twentieth day of February, 1839, the time of its rendezvous at Bangor, Maine, to the twenty-third day of April, 1839, when discharged or mustered.

CAPTAIN.
Daniel Dority.

LIEUTENANT.
John P. Wood.

ENSIGN.
Joseph Eaton.

SERGEANTS.
Henry Noyes.
Nathaniel K. Sawyer.
Ichabod Grindle.
Benjamin Bolton, Jr.
Hiram Haynes.

CORPORALS.
Solomon V. Jones.
William A. Swift.
Charles W. Buckmore.
Amasa T. Patterson.
Credepher Gray.

MUSICIANS.
Josiah H. Emerson.
Spencer Hopkins.
Joram Nichols.

PRIVATES.

Abbott, Moses.
Allen, Stephen W.
Bassick, Samuel.
Blodget, Hiram.
Brier, Robert, Jr.
Brooks, Joseph.
Calef, Daniel.
Cayton, James.
Chase, Hiram.
Cofran, Franklin.
Colson, Theophilus, 2d.
Coombs, James W.
Cross, Joseph.
Cunningham, James.
Cunningham, James.
Cunningham, James O.
Cunningham, William.
Daniels, George D.
Day, Charles.
Durham, Albert.
Eaton, John C.
Edwards, John.
Emerson, Calvin.
Emerson, Joshua L.

George, Samuel T.
Gray, Judson.
Greeley, George.
Grindle, Ezra.
Grindle, Reuben, Jr.
Grindle, Robert.
Gulliver, Benjamin.
Hanson, Albert.
Henderson, Thomas H.
Herrick, Otis W.
Howe, Henry L.
Jones, Nathaniel.
Knowles, Jonathan.
Knowlton, John W.
Knox, Thomas J.
Lancaster, Valentine R.
Larrabee, Josiah A.
Larrabee, Simeon.
Luckings, Thomas P.
Maker, Robert.
Mason, Andrew.
Morgan, Edward.
Patterson, Frederick A.
Patterson, John.

Patterson, Lewis A.
Philbrook, Luther G.
Pike, Henry.
Pote, Robert P.
Potter, James S.
Rand, Marshall H.
Rinds, Joseph S.
Roberts, Cyrus.
Rollins, Owen S.
Sawyer, James H.
Shirley, Christopher.
Shuman, John.
Shuman, Simon.
Smart, John B.
Snow, Richard.
Stephens, George A.
Stimpson, Edwin E.
Swett, Henry L.
Whitcomb, Eben.
Whittier, Elias.
Wilson, William F.
Worthin, Isaac.
Young, William L.

Muster Roll of Captain Sampson Dunham's Company of Infantry in the Detachment of drafted Militia of Maine, called into actual service by the State, for the protection of its Northeastern Frontier, from the sixth day of March, 1839, the time of its rendezvous at Augusta, Maine, to the twenty-ninth day of March, 1839, when discharged or mustered.

CAPTAIN.	LIEUTENANT.	ENSIGN.
Sampson Dunham.	Levi Lunt.	Joseph Field.
SERGEANTS.	CORPORALS.	MUSICIANS.
Harrison Whitman.	Jabez Sawyer.	Alanson M. Whitmore.
William P. Hammon.	Ezekiel L. Porter.	
Alanson Briggs.	Alfred Chase.	
Jonathan Clark.	Asia Mayhew.	
	PRIVATES.	
Allen, David.	Dillingham, Eben H.	Pool, Calvin.
Annis, John G.	France, Sylvanus B.	Robbins, Oliver, 2d.
Banks, Daniel.	Fuller, Alonzo.	Robinson, Alden.
Barbour, Levi.	Hall, Henry S.	Rounds, Ephraim.
Billings, Dexter.	Hawkins, John F.	Smith, Simon.
Blake, Charles.	Mayhew, Abijah.	Spaulding, Sydney.
Bowker, Cyprian.	Millet, Samuel T.	Sturtevant. Thomas.
Brackett, Dexter W.	Noyes, James C.	Tarbox, Ephraim.
Chase, Eleazer.	Paine, Jacob.	Thurston, Elem.
Churchill, James.	Parker, William.	Tobin, Mathew.
Clark, Hezekiah C.	Peterson, Israel R.	Tuptle, Isaac.
Colburn, Jarathaneal.	Pollard, Ezekiel.	Whitmore, Cyprian.
Dammon, Ezekiel.	Pollard, Sylvanus.	Varney, John, Jr.
Davis, Eliphalet.	Pond, Daniel, Jr.	

AROOSTOOK WAR.

Muster Roll of Captain Josiah L. Elder's Company of Infantry in the Detachment of drafted Militia of Maine, called into actual service by the State, for the protection of its Northeastern Fronier, from the sixth day of March, 1839, the time of its rendezvous at Augusta, Maine, to the twenty-ninth day of March, 1839, when discharged or mustered.

CAPTAIN.	LIEUTENANT.	ENSIGN.
Josiah L. Elder.	Nathaniel Stone.	Abram A. Barker.
SERGEANTS.	CORPORALS.	MUSICIANS.
Ebenezer F. Mansfield.	Ichabod Warren.	Mial Jordan.
William H. Powers.	Samuel B. Hadley.	
Dudley Bean, Jr.	Timothy McIntire.	
James W. Downing.	Stephen Weeks.	
	PRIVATES.	
Babb, Libbens H.	Gilman, John.	Richardson, Oliver.
Boobier, Rufus.	Hodgdon, George.	Staples, John H.
Boston, John T.	Kennison, George F.	Stevens, Edmund.
Brown, Simon.	Kimball, Reuben.	Stewart, Samuel, Jr.
Chadbourne, John W.	Littlefield, Charles.	Storer, Horace.
Charles, Farnham.	Lord, Abram.	Taylor, Dean.
Cole, Ira.	Marston, Eben.	Thompson, Phineas.
Cole, Sylvanus.	Marston, Henry.	Thompson, Samuel.
Davidson, George.	Merrifield, Ivory.	Walker, Orrin.
Downs, Daniel.	Ordway, Henry.	Warren, George D.
Farrington, Moses C.	Ordway, John.	Whales, John.
Farrington, Stillman.	Osgood, Charles S.	Witham, Pelatiah.
Fox, Edmund.	Pearl, Isaac.	Wood, Stephen.
Fulsom, John.	Pearl, John E.	

Muster Roll of Captain Nathan Ellis, Jr's., Company of Light Infantry in the Detachment of drafted Militia of Maine, called into actual service by the State, for the protection of its Northeastern Frontier, from the twentieth day of February, 1839, the time of its rendezvous at Bangor, Maine, to the twenty-second day of April, 1839, when discharged or mustered.

CAPTAIN.
Nathan Ellis, Jr.

ENSIGN.
Jeremiah Burnham.

ENSIGN.
James Dunning.

SERGEANTS.
John Pray.
James Littlefield.
Phineas Batchelder.
James H. Stewart.

CORPORALS.
Horace I. Gould.
Frederick K. Bartlett.
Hiram G. Caridge.
George W. McFarland.

MUSICIANS.
Frederic Stewart.
Rufus Smith.

PRIVATES.

Bragg, James.
Brown, John.
Brown, Josiah.
Brown, Perkins.
Burnham, Royal R.
Butterfield, Orrin.
Buzzell, Jonathan.
Chadbourne, Benjamin.
Champion, John.
Clark, Samuel.
Cookson, John.
Corson, Erastus.
Cottle, Samuel F.
Cumston, Robert M.
Daggett, Ebenezer.
Daniels, James M.
Dorr, Barzillai.
Douglass, Israel.
Fitts, Andrew G.

Ferguson, Oliver.
Fogg, Peleg.
Fullerton, George W.
Geral, Daniel.
Glidden, John.
Gordon, Ebenezer H.
Gribbin, Peter R.
Harris, Jairus.
Holt, Samuel H.
Horn, James.
Jellison, Derry P.
Jones, Stephen.
Kelley, Charles.
Longley, Asa.
Martin, Henry B.
Moores, William.
Morey, Solomon.
Myrick, Nathaniel.
Overlock, Christopher.

Overlock, Martin.
Paine, George.
Palmer, William H.
Peavey, Hiram.
Peavey, Jonathan.
Philbrook, Jason R.
Pilsbury, Peter.
Puffer, John.
Roberts, Samuel.
Seaman, Alfred.
Sinclair, Joseph P.
Sprague, Charles S.
Stavers, Charles.
Turner, William.
Wadleigh, Eli.
Wakefield, Paul P.
Ward, Calvin.
Wentworth, Nathaniel S.
White, Nathaniel.

AROOSTOOK WAR. 41

Muster Roll of **Captain Samuel L. Fish's** Company of Infantry in the Detachment of drafted Militia of Maine, called into actual service by the State, for the protection of its Northeastern Frontier, from the twentieth day of February, 1839, the time of its rendezvous at Bangor, Maine, to the twenty-third day of April, 1839, when discharged or mustered.

CAPTAIN.
Samuel L. Fish.

SERGEANTS.
David C. Jellison.
John P. Davis.
Moses S. Page.
Joseph Budson.
James S. Eldridge.
Jesse Hutchins.

Abbot, Thomas.
Abbot, Willard.
Ames, Almarin.
Bachelder, William.
Ballard, William, Jr.
Billings, David L.
Boyd, John.
Burns, George.
Burton, Timothy.
Buzzell, Isaac.
Carr, Justus S.
Chapman, Garey.
Chapman, William I.
Cunningham, Thomas.
Deering, Samuel.
Dickinson, James.
Dorr, Ephraim.
Dunham, John, Jr.
Duran Joseph.
Dwelley, William, Jr.
Eveleth, Elisha M.

LIEUTENANT.
Francis I. Cumming.

CORPORALS.
Josiah McPheters.
Charles H. Forbes.
Joseph Bray.
George Lincoln.
John B. Bond.
Kenney Snow.

PRIVATES.
Emerton, Amasa S.
Ferren, Chester.
Fowles, Daniel.
Gillmore, James H.
Gray, Shadrach.
Grindel, John.
Guppy, William P.
Harmon, Abial.
Holt, Seth.
James, Joseph.
Jordan, Abel S.
Kilburn, Levi R.
Knowlton, Gilbert.
Lancaster, David.
Lassell, William.
Lawrence, John N.
Lawrence, Roland.
Mann, Thomas.
Miller, John E.
Moody, William B.
Montgomery, Henry.

ENSIGN.
Gilbert Emerson.

MUSICIANS.
Robert P. Chase.
Solomon P. Row.

Newcomb, Charles.
Osgood, Alva.
Park, Roderick R.
Patten, Charles.
Pierce, Samuel.
Priest, Joseph.
Raymond, Thomas.
Sheet, Samuel.
Simpson, Jacob.
Snow, William C.
Southard, John, Jr.
Spencer, Samuel.
Stinson, Horatio N.
Stinson, Joseph C.
Stubbs, James.
Swett, Jacob P.
Tapley, Timothy C.
Tower, Levi.
Trevett, Samuel S.
Wood, Benson D.

Muster Roll of Captain Nathaniel Frost's Company of Infantry in the Detachment of drafted Militia of Maine, called into active service by the State, for the protection of its Northeastern Frontier, from the twenty-fifth day of February, 1839, the time of its rendezvous at Augusta, Maine, to the sixteenth day of April, 1839, when discharged or mustered.

CAPTAIN.	LIEUTENANT.	ENSIGN.
Nathaniel Frost.	Gustavus Clark.	George Woodcock.
SERGEANTS.	CORPORALS.	MUSICIANS.
Greenwood Rollins.	Sewall Page.	Hiram Towle.
Walker Chamberlain.	Rhodney Jacobs.	Willard B. Thayer.
Owen Getchell.	William D. Branch.	
Zalmon Sawtelle.	Samuel Wade.	
	PRIVATES.	
Austin, James.	Gowell, John.	Packard, Sewall.
Bartlett, Cyrus.	Gowell, John, Jr.	Packard, Reuben.
Bickford, Almond.	Harmon, Edward.	Pinkham, William.
Bickford, Joseph H.	Hatch, Benjamin.	Pray, Reuben.
Blake, Wade.	Hersom, John, 2d.	Stetson, Henry.
Chandler, Harlow.	Howard, Cyril.	Sawtelle, Charles K.
Chandler, Thomas.	Harmon, Edward.	Stephens, Nathan G.
Clough, Jacob.	Hatch, Benjamin.	Taylor, Elias, 3d.
Damren, Joel T.	Knox, Stephen.	Taylor, John B.
Dyer, Selden.	Moore, Daniel J.	Thayer, Solomon.
Ellis, Freeman.	Mills, Ruel.	Townsend, Joshua.
	Prime, Hiram.	Trask, Samuel.

AROOSTOOK WAR. 43

Additional Roll of Lieutenant William Frost's Company of Infantry in the Detachment of drafted Militia of Maine, called into actual service by the State, for the protection of its Northeastern Frontier, from the twentieth day of February, 1839, the time of its rendezvous at......, Maine, to the fourth day of March, 1839, when discharged or mustered.

CAPTAIN.
Samuel L. Fish.

Henry Noyes.

QUARTERMASTER DEPT.
*Fred'k K. Bartlett.

Levi Emerson.
Thompson Dyer.
Robert Johnson.
Nathan F. Herrick.
William L. Johnson.
Charles Wyman.
David C. Jellison.
Eli Cook.
Elbridge G. Rose.

Dunham, Othuiel.
Harriman, Joab.

LIEUTENANT.
William Frost.

ORDERLY SERGEANTS.
Daniel S. Peters.
Samuel P. Leighton.

SERGEANTS.
Isaac Hills, 2d.
Jesse Hutchins.
Rufus B. Googins.
Horatio Pratt.
William McE. Brown.
David Densmore.
*Levi O. Farnham.
Daniel Shepley.
Ephraim E. Harriman.
Jacob Ingalls, Jr.

PRIVATES.
Herrick, Arthur.
Johnson, William.
Newbit, Alden.

ADJUTANT.
Francis J. Cummings.

Charles H. Connor.

CORPORAL.
*Levi O. Farnham.

Milton Twitchell.
I. S. Eldridge.
Stephen S. Gerrish.
Benj. F. Tozier.
Albert G. Hunt.
George P. Logan.
*Fred'k K. Bartlett.
Caleb Ginn.
Dustan Page.

Porter, Charles.
Saunders, Nathaniel.

Muster Roll of Captain John Gardner's Company of Infantry in the Detachment of drafted Militia of Maine, called into actual service by the State, for the protection of its Northeastern Frontier, from the twenty-fifth day of February, 1839, the time of its rendezvous at Augusta, Maine, to the seventeeth day of April, 1839, when mustered.

CAPTAIN.	LIEUTENANT.	ENSIGN.
John Gardner.	Kendall H. K. Stone.	James B. Lamb.
SERGEANTS.	CORPORALS.	MUSICIANS.
Samuel M. Woodman.	William H. Whittier.	....
Joseph Smith.	Samuel Jackson.	
Alpheus R. Hale.	Charles Spear, Jr.	
Edmund Phillips.	Nathan Kimball.	
	PRIVATES.	
Bessey, Alexander H.	Huntington, Benj. G.	Page, Nathaniel.
Blodgett, Horace.	Lane, John W.	Page, Lewis.
Blackwell, Sylvanus.	Lewis, James B.	Snow, David.
*Clark, Abram.	Lyon, Peter.	Thomas, John W.
Dyle, Edmund.	Maxim, Jacob, Jr.	Towle, Henry W.
Foster, Charles S.	Maxim, Thomas.	Wing, George W.
Foss, Walter.	Mariner, James H.	Woodcock, Hannibal H.
Graves, Sewall H.		

*Clock, Abram.

AROOSTOOK WAR.

Muster Roll of Captain Zachariah Gibson's Company of Artillery in the Detachment of drafted Militia of Maine, called into actual service by the State, for the protection of its Northeastern Frontier, from the sxth day of March, 1839, the time of its rendezvous at Augusta, Maine, to the twenty-seventh day of March, 1839, when discharged or mustered.

CAPTAIN.
Zachariah Gibson.

LIEUTENANTS.
Jesse Bradford, 1st.
Benajmin Maxim, 2d.
Seth Beale, Jr., 2d.

SERGEANTS.
Sylvanus B. Bean.
Hannibal Thompson.
Chandler F. Millet.
James Weeks, Jr.

CORPORALS.
Nelson Cushman.
Thomas Cary.
Henry Jones.
Atwell Richardson.

MUSICIANS.
Amasa Johnson.
Elijah Tebbetts.
Horace Cushman.

PRIVATES.
Alden, Benjamin Jr.
Alden, Columbus.
Alden, Loren.
Beals, Hiram.
Bennett, Andrew.
Blake, Caleb.
Bray, Ebenezer.
Briggs, Daniel H.
Bryant, Otis.
Byram, Orville.
Coburn, Frederick, Jr.
Cushman, Alden.
Cushman, Jonathan.
Daggett, John.
Daniels, Joseph.
Dennett, Mark.
Downing, Moses.
Dunlap, Elbridge.
Dyer, Daniel Y.
Felton, Jonathan W.
Fish, Sanford.
Fisk, Alden B.
Gossom, William.
Hackett, Daniel.
Hall, Lyman N.
Hill, Daniel H.
Jones, Edson.
Jones, James.
Jones, William H.
Keene, Gaius.
Larrabee, Ammi.
Mansfield, Stephen P.
Marson, Isaac.
Martin, John.
Morrill, Nicholas D.
Peterson, Benjamin, Jr.
Pike, Dudley.
Poor, William, Jr.
Ricker, Bradford W.
Rose, Emerson.
Soule, Benjamin.
Stiles, Isaac.
Stanley, John.
Strout, David.
Tubs, Elias A.
Weeks, Napoleon.
Wentworth, Cyrus.

AROOSTOOK WAR.

Muster Roll of Captain **Isaac Greene's** Company of Infantry in the Detachment of drafted Militia of Maine, called into actual service by the State, for the protection of its Northeastern Frontier, from the sixth day of March, 1839, the time of its rendezvous at Calais, Maine, to the fifth day of April, 1839, when discharged or mustered.

CAPTAIN.	LIEUTENANT.	ENSIGN.
Isaac Greene.	Jesse Flood.	Albert Treworgy.

SERGEANTS.	CORPORALS.	MUSICIANS.
John C. Macomber.	Ruel Bartlett.	John Ames.
Solomon I. Treworgy.	Spofford P. Thomas.	
Ichabod Kent.	Joseph Kelliher.	
Isaac Frazier, Jr.	John Frazier.	

PRIVATES.

Bowden, John.	Higgins, Asa.	Ober, Nicholas.
Cook, Hezekiah.	Higgins, Jesse, Jr.	Remmick, Philip.
Cook, John.	Higgins, Joseph M.	Rich, John.
Cousins, Joseph N.	Hill, Leroy.	Salisbury, Calvin.
Creamer, Gardner.	Hodgdon, Thomas.	Sanders, Edward.
Cripps, Josiah.	Hopkins, Enoch.	Sanders, Richard.
Cunningham, Anson.	Ingalls, Daniel.	Somersby, Jacob.
Curtis, Paul.	Jones, Jr., Charles.	Stephens, James.
Curtis, Uzziel.	Knight, Warren.	Swett, Roswell.
Dendico, Sewall.	Lee, William.	Tourtilotte, Elisha.
Emery, Hiram W.	Leach, Josiah B.	Tourtilotte, Joshua.
Flood, Thomas N.	Liscomb, Gideon.	Townsend, William.
Floyd, Jeremiah.	MacPheters, Prentice P.	Treworgy, George.
Frazier, Samuel.	Martin, Lewis.	Varnum, Benjamin.
Garland, David.	Milliken, Benjamin.	Varnum, Samuel.
Garland, John.	Moore, Ezekiel W.	Wentworth, Jonah.
Giles, Benjamin.	Moore, John.	Wilson, John.
Green, Jonas.	Morgan, Asa G.	Young, Edwin.
Hadley, William R.	Murch, Cyrus.	Young, Ellis.
Haskell, John T.	Murch, John L.	

Muster Roll of Captain Joshua T. Hall's Company of Infantry in the Detachment of drafted Militia of Maine, called into actual service by the State, for the protection of its Northeastern Frontier, from the sixth day of March, 1839, the time of its rendezvous at Augusta, Maine, to the twenty-ninth day of March, 1839, when discharged or mustered.

CAPTAIN. Joshua T. Hall.	LIEUTENANT.	ENSIGN. John C. Stockbridge.
SERGEANTS. John M. Adams. John B. Holman. Ebenezer Hutchinson. George K. Smith.	CORPORALS. Enoch Stiles. George A. Ray. Martin Ellis, Jr. John W. Dearbon.	MUSICIANS. Rathons B. Waite. Albert G. Glines.
Abbott, Horatio N. Andrews, James. Andrews, William. Bailey, William. Bartlett, Jonathan A. Boynton, James S. Brackett, Simeon. Dolby, George. Elliot, Abner H. French, William R.	PRIVATES. Frost, William P. Hall, Kimball. Hardy, Asa. Hutchins, Enos A. Jennings, Abiathar I. Lamb, James. Lovejoy, Azel. Lufkin, Aaron H. McKenney, Silas. Noyes, Ezra.	Rich, Luther. Royal, Rufus S. Shackley, John. Stevens, Benjamin W. Taintor, Alsworth. Tucker, Elbridge. Virgin, Stephen. Winter, John. Young, Hiram.

Muster Roll of Captain Charles R. Hamblet's Company of Infantry in the Detachment of drafted Militia of Maine, called into actual service by the State, for the protection of its Northeastern Frontier, from the twentieth day of February, 1839, the time of its rendezvous at Bangor, Maine, to the twenty-fifth day of April, 1839, when discharged or mustered.

CAPTAIN.
Charles R. Hamblet.

LIEUTENANT.
Amasa R. Walker.

ENSIGN.
John Nelson.

SERGEANTS.
Elbridge H. Bragdon, (O.S)
Benjamin M. Page.
Attilius Ladd.
Samuel F. Eells.

CORPORALS.
Elias Harriman.
Barzillia Huckins.
Benjamin C. Sanders.
William W. Burnham.
Sabin H. Kimball.

MUSICIANS.
....

PRIVATES.

Ames, Amariah W.
Annis, Joseph S.
Appleton, William.
Bailey, Daniel.
Barney, William.
Beals, Samuel.
Bean, Daniel.
Bradley, Thomas.
Brooks, Daniel.
Burgess, Thomas A.
Bucks, Ira B.
Capers, Nathaniel.
Card, Thornton.
Carter, Jonathan.
Carver, James.
Chase, John.
Chase, Joseph C.
Crocker, Freeman.
Crocker, Henry.
Crocker, Moses.
Dexter, Isaac.

Dow, Stephen.
Farnham, Levi O.
Fish, Nathaniel B.
Gerry, Ebenezer O.
Gordon, John.
Gould, Isaac.
Hanscomb, Nathaniel.
Hawes, Christopher.
Homes, Ezra.
Howard, Daniel.
Knox, John.
Larrabee, Hiram.
Leathers, Tuttle D.
Lee, James.
Lothrop, Orman F.
Maddocks, Walter D.
McKenney, William.
Minor, Lyman.
Mitchell, Samuel.
Newcomb, Stillman.
Rider, Isaac.

Rich, Peter J.
Roberts, Nathaniel D.
Rogers, George W.
Rose, Joseph.
Royal, Silas.
Sampson, George R.
Severance, Seth.
Shepherd, William.
Sibley, Henry.
Simpson, Wells.
Stevens, William C.
Tilton, Joseph.
Trask, William.
Wallon, Alexander D.
Washburn, Ira.
Webb, Thomas.
West, James.
Whittemore, Nelson.
Whittemore, Simon.
Wilkinson, Levi M.
Woodward, John.
Young, Albert R.

AROOSTOOK WAR. 49

Muster Roll of Lieutenant Hiram Hamilton's Company of Infantry in the Detachment of drafted Militia of Maine, called into actual service by the State, for the protection of its Northeastern Frontier, from the twenty-fifth day of February, 1839, the time of its rendezvous at Augusta, Maine, to the twenty-first day of April, 1839, when disdischarged or mustered.

CAPTAIN.	LIEUTENANT. Hiram Hamilton.	ENSIGN. Benjamin Adams.
SERGEANTS. James N. Randlett. Benjamin Clough. John M. Maxwell. William C. Bates. Edwin Turner.	CORPORALS. Alfred Hamilton. Joseph P. Rowell. Seth Fogg. Simeon C. Mower.	MUSICIANS.
Arno, Hiram. Arno, John. Bessey. Jonathan B. Boynton, James M. Chadbourne, Josiah. Clark, Robert H. Cowan, Levi, Jr. Fogg, Alvan. Gove, Jonathan. Gray, William C. Groves, Henry.	PRIVATES. Grover, John. Hackett, Amos. Hackett, Ezekiel. Hackett, Joseph. Hackett, Samuel. Hall, Joseph. Ham, Joel. Jackman, Sewall. McFarland, David. McFarland, James. Murch, Aaron, Jr.	Peare, Moses. Prescott, Eli L. Prescott, Stephen A. Potter, Elijah R. Randlett, Samuel M. Smith, James S. F. Starbird, Luther. Warren, Enoch S. Wight, Milton M. Wing, Alexander.

4

Muster Roll of Captain William S. Haines' Company of Infantry in the Detachment of drafted Militia of Maine, called into actual servce by the State, for the protection of its Northeastern Fronter, from the twenty-fifth day of Februay, 1839, the time of its rendezvius at Augusta, Maine, to the nineteenth day of April, 1839, when discharged or mustered.

CAPTAIN.	LIEUTENANT.	ENSIGN.
William S. Haines.	Thomas Hovey.	......
SERGEANTS.	CORPORALS.	MUSICIANS.
Abner Pitts, Jr.	Eliphalet Rollins.	Silas Hunt.
Alexander T. Katon.	Asa Trask.	
F. M. Collier.	John Tarr.	
William Thornton, Jr.	Nathan Swetland.	
	PRIVATES.	
Austin, Jesse.	Cummings, Moses C.	Minor, Dwight.
Beedle, William.	Davis, Moses.	Moody, Charles.
Booker, James.	Emerson, Benjamin D.	Moody, Lewis.
Brown, Abial.	Gray, Samuel.	Moody, John.
Bunker, Rufus.	Heath, Jacob.	Norton, Joseph F.
Christopher, William.	Holbrook, Thomas W.	Potter, James W.
Collins, William H.	Little, William, Jr.	Rollins, T. W.
Covell, John.	Lyon, George W.	Stacy, William H.
Crocker, Samuel.	McKenney, Charles.	Stevens, Hiram B.

AROOSTOOK WAR. 51

Muster Roll of Captain James C. Harper's Company of Infantry in the Detachment of drafted Militia of Maine, called into actual service by the State, for the protection of its Northeastern Frontier, from the sixth day of March, 1839, the time of its rendezvous at Augusta, Maine, to the twenty-eigth day of March 1839, when discharged or mustered.

CAPTAIN.	LIEUTENANT.	ENSIGN.
James C. Harper.	John Hutchinson.	Merrill Holman.
SERGEANTS.	CORPORALS.	MUSICIANS.
Reuben P. Brown.	David Tucker.	Emerson Pitts.
Reuben Townsend.	Philip Abbott.	Amasa Alden.
Orin Huntress.	Jonathan S. Berry.	
Joseph N. Masterman.	Phanuel White.	

	PRIVATES.	
Bartlett, Joseph.	Holt, Herman.	Rollins, Axel I.
Bradeen, Isaac.	Kenerson, Bryant.	Russell, Philo E.
Chase, Elbridge.	Keys, Oliver.	Sawtelle, Edwin.
Crockett, John, Jr.	Kidder, Augustus.	Smith, Madison.
Delanoe, Charles G.	Leach, Gideon.	Starbird, Watson R.
Deluce, Joseph H.	Lothrop, Leonard.	Stevens, Francis.
Dike, William.	Lovejoy, Christopher.	Sturdivant, Lott.
Farnham, Joseph A.	Merrill, Ansel.	Thayer, Solomon.
Fogg, Ezekiel F.	Mitchell, Henry.	Thompson, Alonzo.
French, Gideon.	Nash, John E.	Thomas, Elbridge G.
Frost, Alden B.	Newton, Estes.	Timberlake, Silas.
Fuller, Albion P.	Newton, Jacob F.	Tobin, Joseph, Jr.
Fuller, Samuel, Jr.	Parker, Jonathan.	White, John.
Gibos, Franklin.	Pierce, Asa.	White, John, 2d.
Gross, William, Jr.	Pinkham, Joseph.	Whitmore, William C.
Hathaway, Columbus.	Raymond, Solomon.	Wood, William.
Holt, Erastus.	Reed, Amaziah.	

Muster Roll of Captain David H. Haskell's Company of Infantry in the Detachment of drafted Militia of Maine, called into actual service by the State, for the protection of its Northeastern Frontier, from the sixth day of March, 1839, the time of its rendezvous at Augusta, Maine, to the twenty-eight day of March, 1839, when discharged or mustered.

CAPTAIN.
David H. Haskell.

LIEUTENANT.
....

ENSIGN.
Sumner Frost.

SERGEANTS.
Solomon Bisbee.
George Russell.
Amos Flint.
Robert Gray.

CORPORALS.
Samuel Brown, Jr.
John L. Cummings.
Columbus Holden.
James Brickett.

MUSICIANS.
Walter L. Bryant.
Daniel Clark.

Abbott, William W.
Abbott, Freeman F.
Andrews, Thaddeus B.
Baker, Luke, Jr.
Bassett, James.
Bell, John, 3d.
Billings, John D.
Bisbee, Charles.
Brown, Francis D.
Butters, Sewall.
Coffin, Daniel.
Davis, Sylvanus G.
Day, Thomas.
Evans, James.
Foster, Edmund W.
Gray, John.

PRIVATES.
Greene, John A.
Greene, William.
Hamlin, Eleazer.
Hale, Albion K. P.
Hartford, James.
Hasselton, Joshua.
Horne, Isaac.
Johnson, David.
Kimball, David.
Kneeland, Ebenezer.
Kneeland, Ephraim W.
Knight, James.
Libby, Walter.
Libby, William.
Lord, Richard.
Marshall, William.

McDaniels, Dean.
Nelson, Oliver.
Randall, Samuel, 3d.
Robinson, Alfred.
Sampson, Amos.
Stearns, Absalom.
Stearns, Timothy.
Stone, Alonzo.
Wardwell, Isaac.
Webb, Daniel.
Weston, Zachariah.
Wood, Borden.
Woodman, Ariel L.
York, John.

Muster Roll of Captain S. A. Holbrook's Company of Light Infantry in Detachment of drafted Militia of Maine, called into actual service by the State, for the protection of its Northeastern Frontier, from the sixth day of March, 1839, the time of its rendezvous at Augusta, Maine, to the twenty-sixth day of March, 1839, when discharged or mustered.

CAPTAIN.
S. A. Holbrook.

SERGEANTS.
Robert P. Kendall.
McKeen Johnson.
Hooper D. Strout.
Jere H. Moore.

Allen, Joseph.
Andrews, Robert R.
Barker, Jonathan.
Barstow, Hetherty.
Berry, Isaac.
Brown, James.
Chase, Samuel Q.
Churchill, Matthew.
Cobb, John.
Cobb, Reuben S.
Cobb, Stephen.
Draper, Richard.
Elder, William S.
Emerson, Emery.
Ferguson, Nathan.
Fitzgerild, Henry C.
Gibson, Parker.
Gilman, Eben.
Grant, Unite.
Greene, George W.

LIEUTENANT.
John F. Sawyer.

CORPORALS.
Theo L. Curtis.
Peroz I. Griffin.
Gustavus Rogers.
John H. Tuttle.

PRIVATES.
Greene, Rufus.
Goddard, Edward.
Gore, John.
Haskell, Moses.
Hawkes, Edward P.
Hawkes, James R.
Holmes, Stewart.
Humphrey, Benjamin, Jr.
Jordan, Benjamin R.
Latham, Artemas.
Latham, J. Ezra.
Libby, Cyrus J.
Loring, George.
Maxwell, Moses.
McIntosh, John.
Nash, James.
Page, Dennis.
Purington, Fred.
Richards, Curtis C.
Robert, Charles.

ENSIGN.
Timothy H. Weymouth.

MUSICIANS.
James Frank, Jr.
Henry Cummings.

Robinson, Elijah.
Sawyer, Reuben A.
Skillings, William.
Smith, William.
Spiller, Alpheus.
Staple, Joseph.
Strout, Alonzo.
Swett, Nathan H.
Townsend, James.
Tripp, Jacob.
True, Benjamin.
Turner, Josiah M.
Watson, Joseph.
White, Fred S.
White, Robert.
Woodbury, George B.
Wright, Nathan.
Young, Atwood F. N.
Young, William.
York, William L.

Muster Roll of Captain James Huxford's Company of Light Infantry in the Detachment of drafted Militia of Maine, called into actual service by the State, for the protection of its Northeastern Frontier, from the twentieth day of February, 1839, the time of its rendezous at Bangor, Maine, to the twenty-sixth day of April, 1839, when discharged or mustered.

CAPTAIN.
James Huxford.

SERGEANTS.
Sylvanus Eaton.
William Reynolds.
Barzillai W. Lane.
John Penn Pilley.

Batchelder, William.
Bennett, Alanson.
Boobar, Calvin I.
Bowden, Sylvester.
Bunker, Benjamin.
Burton, David.
Carlisle, George W.
Condon, Daniel.
Cotton, Horace.
Curtis, Ezra.
Dodge, Sabbina.
Door, John E.
Douglass, James.
Fogg, John H.
Fogg, William L.
Ford, Moses.
Frost, Enoch.
Garland, Ebenezer.
Gerrish, Nathaniel.
Gilman, Enoch W.
Gray, Alexander.
Green, Asa.

LIEUTENANT.
Francis Thorndike.

CORPORALS.
Benjamin Cilley.
Erastus Lane.
Charles H. Thorndike.
Nathaniel Boynton.

PRIVATES.
Gross, Joseph.
Gross, John.
Guptill, William.
Hall, Arthur.
Hanson, Levi.
Hardin, Marshal.
Herrick, Jeremiah H.
Higgins, Jesse.
Holtt, Samuel P.
Hubbard, John H.
Ingalls, Nahum H.
Jackson, Oren.
Jones, Lebbeus.
Johnson, Kimball.
Kenney, Isaac S.
Keys, Otis.
Kimball, Thomas.
Lawrence, Daniel.
Leathers, Benjamin.
Lowell, Ebenezer.
Mathews, William.
McLane, Daniel.

ENSIGN.
Benjamin Rowe.

MUSICIANS.
Isaac Fogg.
Lucius Huxford.
Thomas A. Herrick.
Orrington Smith.

Mead, James.
Nesmith, Isaac C.
Oakes, Ebenezer G.
Osgood, Fred P.
Osgood, Isaac.
Parker, Amasa W.
Patten, Michael H.
Partridge, Francis.
Perkins, Ephraim M
Rich, Franklin.
Rich, Oliver T.
Roberts, Benjamin.
Roberts, Winslow.
Rowe, Learned.
Smith, Amos.
Stetson, Nahum.
Saunders, Silas.
Thompson, Emery.
Watts, Samuel.
Webb, Edward.
Worthing, William P.
Young, Alfred.

AROOSTOOK WAR.

Muster Roll of Captain John D. Kinsman's Company of Riflemen in the Detachment of drafted Militia of Maine, called into actual service by the State, for the protection of its Northeastern Frontier, from the sixth day of March, 1839, the time of its endezvous at Augusta, Maine, to the twenty-sixth day of March, 1839, when discharged or mustered.

CAPTAIN.
John D. Kinsman.

LIEUTENANT.
Randolph A. L. Codman.

ENSIGN.
Daniel F. Allen.

SERGEANTS.
Lincoln Radford.
Daniel F. Allen.
Benjamin W. Doe.
Lathrop L. Crockett.

CORPORALS.
George H. Plummer.
George Gowell.
Asa Greeley, Jr.
William H. Johnson.

MUSICIANS.
Jonas W. Davis.
Elliot Y. Fogg.

PRIVATES.

Abbot, Levi G.
Allen, Isaac N.
Banks, Orrin.
Blake, Daniel P.
Chipman, Hiram.
Clark, Charles M.
Collins, Ebenezer, Jr.
Corson, Frederick F.
Davies, Edward H.
Emery, John W.
Eveleth, Halsey H.
Farr, Converse.
Fox, Daniel Jr.
Freeman, Daniel, Jr.
Gage, Richard.
Gilbert, William H.
Goold, John F.
Gove, Elbridge G.
Gowell, Hiram.

Graffam, C. P.
Grueby, Edward L.
Hammond, George H.
Higgins, William.
Hilton, William H.
Jackman, Aaron.
Jasper, Samuel B.
Kemp, John.
Lovitt, Gardner.
Lunt, John S.
Mitchell, Francis B.
Mitchell, Nathaniel, Jr.
Newell, Samuel.
Parsons, Edwin.
Pennell, Charles.
Pettengill, John.
Pratt, Joseph.
Richardson, Joshua W.
Sawyer, Alfred.

Seavey, James.
Shaw, Edwardus.
Small, Nathan M.
Small, Joseph L.
Smith, Peter B.
Snell, Albion, K. P.
Stevens, Edward P.
Sweetser, Daniel.
Thayer, Simon.
Titcomb, William.
Veriel, William, 3d.
Warren, Amos G.
Welch, Thomas.
Wentworth, George.
Weymouth, David.
Wilbur, John.
Woodbury, Nathan P.
York, Charles E.

Muster Roll of Captain Timothy Ludden's Company of Light Infantry in the Detachment of drafted Militia of Maine, called into actual service by the State, for the protection of its Northeastern Frontier from the sixth day of March, 1839, the time of its rendezvous at Augusta, Maine, to the twenty-seventh day of March, 1839, when discharged or mustered.

CAPTAIN.	LIEUTENANT.	ENSIGN.
Timothy Ludden.	Cyrus Hersey.	William Doble.

SERGEANTS.	CORPORALS.	MUSICIANS.
James Russ.	Lawson Mason.	Etsil G. Smith.
Hiram Wormell.	Leonard Thurlow.	Jacob Witham.
Oliver Perkins.	Charles B. Brooks.	
Edmund Butterfield.	Samuel White, 3d.	

PRIVATES.

Annis, George W.
Bennett, John, Jr.
Benson, Thomas J.
Berry, Mial.
Bragdon, Thomas.
Carter, Amos.
Caswell, John A.
Caswell, Justus.
Chaffin, George G.
Chase, Stephen D.
Crocker, John.
Davidson, John.
DeCoster, Thomas.
Eaton, Ebenezer.
Edwards, James M.
Farnham, David H.
Ford, Benjamin F.

Foster, Hiram.
Fuller, Charles P.
Gammon, William.
Hastings, Gideon A.
Hill, William J.
Howe, Alvin.
Knight, Elmore.
Knight, Lorenzo.
Lawrence, Daniel.
Lovejoy, Joseph.
Lufkin, Lory C.
Masterman, Daniel.
McKusick, Francis.
Merrill, Cyrus.
Mitchell, Silas.
Morse, Seth.
Noyes, Edward H.

Pugsley, Abraham.
Rand, Nahum.
Rankins, Enoch.
Rankins, Perley.
Record, Asa.
Rich, Reuben, Jr.
Spaulding, Benjamin F.
Smith, Ephraim P.
Smith, Peter.
Swan, Orrin B.
Trumbull, Foster.
Twitchell, Ozman.
Walker, Daniel.
Warren, John.
Wentworth, William.
Witham, Pelatiah.
Yeaton, Daniel B.

AROOSTOOK WAR. 57

Muster Roll of Captain Stephen Leighton, Jr's. Company of Riflemen in the Detachment of drafted Militia of Maine, called into actual service by the State, for the protection of its Northeastern Frontier, from the twentieth day of February, 1839 the time of its rendezvous at Bangor, Maine, to the twenty-second day of April, 1839, when discharged or mustered.

CAPTAIN.
Stephen Leighton, Jr.

LIEUTENANT.
Isaiah Beals.

ENSIGN
Alvin B. Clark.

SERGEANTS.
Reuben Flanders.
Hiram Safford.
Asa Spooner.
Seth Drew.

CORPORALS.
Stephen D. Jennings.
Charles Jumper.
Cyrus Jumper.
Calvin Safford.

MUSICIANS.
John M. Shaw.

Abbott, Willard.
Arnold, Lemuel.
Barden, Othniel.
Bedee, Isaac.
Berry, David.
Bosworth, William, Jr.
Bridge, Levi, Jr.
Brown, Benjamin, Jr.
Brown, David G.
Brown, Reuben.
Brown, William McE.
Burleigh, James P.
Cole, John.
Copeland, Gardner.
Crowell, James.
Cushman, Ellis.
Day, Andrew N.
Densmore, David.
Dyer, Thompson.
Emerson, Levi.
Fish, Stephen.
Gould, Joseph.
Grindell, David R. W.

PRIVATES.
Hillman, Samuel.
Hodsdon, Charles M.
Howard, Daniel H.
Hunt, Albert G.
Ireland, Benjamin.
Jennings, Charles.
Johnson, Robert.
Johnson, William L.
Jumper, William.
Kimball, John.
Lane, James.
Leavitt, John.
Leavitt, Silas.
Leighton, Seba F.
Logan, Charles R.
Logan, George P.
Longley, Edward P.
Oakes, George.
Palmer, Daniel.
Pickering, Isaac H.
Pitcher, Jonathan, Jr.
Pratt, Horatio.
Ricker, John.
Safford, John.

Safford, Simeon, Jr.
Sampson, Darius.
Sawyer, Henry K.
Severance, George W.
Shaw, Luther H.
Snow, Henry.
Sprague, Henry A.
Sturtevant, Curtis.
Thoms, Harrison G. O.
Towle, John.
Tozier, Benjamin F.
Treworgy, Charles D.
Tucker, Isaac.
Twitchell, Milton.
Walker, William B.
Wardwell, Burnham.
Wardwell, Ira.
Washburn, Peleg.
Whittemore, George.
Willard, Rufus.
Winslow, Andrew C.
Winslow, Eli.
Wyman, Charles.

Muster Roll of Captain Enoch R. Lumbert's Company of Artillery in the Detachment of drafted Militia of Maine, called into acutal service by the State, for the protection of its Northeastern Frontier, from the twentieth day of February, 1839, the time of its rendezvous at Maine, to the twenty-third day of April, when discharged or mustered.

	CAPTAIN. Enoch R. Lumbert.	
John Quimby.	LIEUTENANTS. Fifield Lyford.	Alfred Kirkpatrick.
Hebron Luce, Ord. Sergt. Daniel M. Haskell. Tristram C. Godding.	SERGEANTS. Luther Rideout. Daniel Webster.	Liberty Drew. Joseph Bartlett. Stephen B. Dockham.
Daniel E. Fifield.	CORPORALS. Micah C. Emerson. Hiram Hawes.	Charles Doble.
Royal H. Batchelder.	MUSICIANS.	Levi M. Perry.
Adams, James W. Bailey, Moody. Bartlett, Zenas. Batchelder, James. Batchelder, John, 2d. Batchelder, Dodge. Bridge, Samuel. Burnham Mark. Chase, Alexander H. Coburn, Jonas. Davis, Andrew S. Davis, Robert P. Downe, Henry A. Doble, Orren. Draper, Hiram. Elliot, Rufus S. Fifield, Thomas B. Gates, Zaloch. Gleason, Dennis.	PRIVATES. Godwin, Hiram F. Goodwin, Enoch P. Gould, Thomas F. Hamilton, Samuel. Haskell, Andrew M. Haskell, Charles. Hawes, Henry. Huff, Benjamin W. Kimball, Jedediah. Knight, Samuel. Leighton, Harvey E. Littlefield, Daniel S. Ladd, John C. Lougee, James. Merriam, Artemas. Miles, Abram. Moulton, Stephen C. Neal, William. Norton, Elijah.	Nute, John. Page, Ezekiel. Patten, James R. Patten, Nathaniel R. Perkins, Robert. Reed, Jeremiah. Runnels, John S. Shackleton, John. Skinner, Albert. Smith, Gardner. Smith, John P. Stinson, Waterman. Tobbin, John. Tomlinson, Paul. Tuttle, Isaac. West, John. Whittier, Amasa. Whittier, Porter, Jr. Webster, Richard, Jr. Warren, James.

AROOSTOOK WAR.   59

Muster Roll of Captain Eliphalet L. Maxfield's Company of Infantry in the Detachment of drafted Militia of Maine, called into actual service by the State, for the protection of its Northeastern Frontier, from the twentieth day of February, 1839 the time of its rendezvous at Bangor and Lincoln, Maine, to the twenty-fifth day of April, 1839, when discharged or mustered.

CAPTAIN.	LIEUTENANT.	ENSIGN.
Eliphalet I. Maxfield.	Horatio Barrett.	Goodridge Cummings.
SERGEANTS.	**CORPORALS.**	**MUSICIANS.**
Horace Banks.	Alvin Merryfield.	Nathaniel Fellows.
Carlisle Dennis.	Thomas I. Towle.	
Joseph Nelson.	Charles Davis.	
John Abbot.	Walker Darling.	

PRIVATES.

Ayers, Bradley B.	Emery, John B.	McTosh, James G.
Bailey, Daniel.	Emerson, Charles.	McTosh, William H.
Bailey, Philip.	Emerson, Joseph.	Miles, Josiah.
Bazzell, William F.	Emerson, William.	Moody, Carleton P.
Bickford, Enoch W.	Haynes, Stephen P.	Moody, Rufus.
Brown, William.	Heywood, Willmoth.	Morgan, John.
Buck, John W.	Hodgdon, Joseph.	Morrill, Frederic.
Clark, Sherburn W.	Hodgdon, Moses.	Norton, Samuel, Jr.
Comstock, Solomon.	Ingalls, Moses, Jr.	Noyes, Calvin L.
Coombs, Albert.	Jordan, Joseph.	Perkins, Stover.
Cooper, James.	Johnson, William.	Pratt, John.
Dam, Joel F.	Judkins, Benjamin.	Richards, Josiah.
Dam, Leader N.	Kneeland, David.	Rogers, William G.
Damren, Chandler.	Lane, John W.	Sanborn, James.
Davis, Asahel.	Lane, Mathias.	Scott, John.
Davis, David B.	Lankester, Solomon P.	Smart, Charles L.
Deling, James.	Lawton, John.	Smith, Thomas.
Devo, William.	Leavitt, Eliphalet.	Tosh, William A.
Doe, Nahalie.	Lord, Horace.	Tracy, Israel.
Eastman, Benjamin.	Lovett, Alfred S.	Warton, Joshua.
Edgerly, Daniel W.	Merrill, George W.	Weymouth, Mark G.
Elkins, John, Jr.	McPheters, Samuel.	Young, David.

Muster Roll of Captain George W. Maxim's Company of Infantry in the Detachment of drafted Militia of Maine, called into actual service by the State, for the protection of its Northeastern Frontier, from the twentieth day of Fberuary, 1839, the time of its rendezvous at Bangor, Maine, to the twenty-fourth day of April, 1839, when discharged or mustered.

CAPTAIN.
George W. Maxim.

LIEUTENANT.
Jonathan Lowder.

ENSIGN.
William H. Gibbs.

SERGEANTS.
William Averill.
David Getchell.
Daniel Moulton.
Joel Vickery.

CORPORALS.
Dudley D. Bean.
Jeremy Baker.
Jacob Holyoke.
William W. Smith.

MUSICIANS.
Greenleaf M. Fogg.
James G. Patterson.
George S. Herrick.
Francis C. Keisor.

PRIVATES.

Ames, John.
Bagley, Levi.
Blunt, Enoch M.
Buffam, Charles.
Chaplin, Charles E.
Cleveland, James B.
Cook, Seth F.
Cookson, Reuben.
Cowan, John, Jr.
Curtis, Rufus G.
Damon, Joseph B.
Davis, Asa, 2d.
Dillingham, Benjamin.
Fogg, John M.
Francis, Joseph.
Glidden, Ephraim.
Gould, Thomas.
Gullifer, Thomas.
Hamilton, Sumner.
Hatch, William P.

Higgins, Bradford.
Homans, James S.
Houston, Samuel.
Hovey, Manassah S.
Hurd, Manoah.
Ireland, David G.
Jenkins, Thomas.
Johnson, Ephraim.
Littlefield, Robert.
Maynor, Moses.
McCondray, Ephraim B.
McKenney, Isaiah.
Nickerson, Shuber, Jr.
Orff, Simon.
O'Rooke, James.
Page, Norman.
Parsons, John.
Patterson, Samuel.
Peasley, Enoch.
Pratt, Benjamin.

Pratt, George.
Ramsdell, William H.
Riggs, Wilmot.
Rines, Allen.
Russ, Jesse.
Sawyer, Asa.
Sherburn, William, Jr.
Shorey, David.
Sibley, Abram.
Smith, Christopher.
Stiles, Asa L.
Torrance, Levi S.
Torrance, Samuel S.
Weymouth, John.
White, Stephen.
Willey, Daniel.
Williams, Shuber N.
Witham, John.
Young, Francis.

AROOSTOOK WAR. 61

Muster Roll of Captain William H. Mills' Company of Riflmen in the Detachment of drafted Militia of Maine, called into actual service by the State, for the protection of its Northeastern Frontier, from the twentieth day of February, 1839, the time of its rendezvous at Bangor, Maine, to the thirteenth day of May, 1839, when discharged or mustered.

CAPTAIN.
William H. Mills.

LIEUTENANT.
James Henry Carleton.

ENSIGN.
Henry L. Stewart.

SERGEANTS.
Elijah Low, Ord. Sergt.
George A. Longfellow.
Jesse Snow.
Hiram Fogg.

CORPORALS.|
Jason L. Bourne.
Abraham Colomy.
Amos S. Myrick.
Isaac Lunt.

MUSICIANS.
Arthur Heald.
Dennis J. Bither.

Abbot, Samuel.
Adams, James.
Adams, William.
Babcock, John W.
Barrows, Samuel.
Bartlett, Nehemiah.
Batchelder, Daniel.
Burrill, Ziba.
Byram, Erastus B.
Clough, Noah.
Comery, Sandford.
Cousins, William.
Costelow, Samuel W.
Cross, Joseph K.
Davis, Elisha.
Davis, James P.
Davis, James M.
Drew, Lorraine I.
Dunton, Jason.
Emerson, Benjamin.
Farrington, Ebenezer.
Fowles, Asa.

PRIVATES.
French, Lewis R.
Gordon, Joseph.
Gorton, John.
Gorton, James.
Goss, Watson R.
Grindle, Joseph.
Grindle, Simeon B.
Guptil, Benjamin.
Hewes, Stephen S.
Hills, Isaac, 2d.
Hills, Jason.
Hodgkins, Thomas.
House, David B.
Lebroke, Hiram.
Lombard, James A.
McCausland, Thomas.
Miller, David.
Miller, James, Jr.
Miller, Sewall.
Moore, John.
Newcomb, Peter B.
Paine, John.

Pattee, Stephen B.
Patten, Levi B.
Perry, Clark.
Plummer, John A.
Richards, Almon.
Ring, John.
Rogers, James.
Shepley, David.
Springer, Stephen C.
Smith, Sumner.
Stevens, George A.
Stevens, Hiram.
Sturdevant, Francis J.
Sylvester, Joseph T.
Shepley, Daniel C.
Thompson, Jeremiah.
Towne, Eli.
Walker, Samuel F.
Weymouth, Robert H.
Wiley, Charles.
Woodman, Asa.
Young, James.

Muster Roll of Captain Amos F. Noyes' Company of Infantry in the Detachment of drafted Militia of Maine, called into actual service by the State, for the protection of its Northeastern Frontier, from the sixth day of March, 1839, the time of its rendezvous at Augusta, Maine, to the twenty-eighth day of March, 1839, when discharged or mustered.

CAPTAIN.
Amos F. Noyes.

LIEUTENANT.
Abrah Hobbs.

ENSIGN.
Washington French.

SERGEANTS.
Joseph Dearborn.
Nathan K. Noble.
Isaac W. Grant.
William Jordan.

CORPORALS.
Jeremiah Foster.
Phineas Doble.
Ansel Stevens.
Nathaniel Sampson.

MUSICIAN.
James S. Greenleaf.

PRIVATES.

Bancroft, Daniel M.
Benson, James S.
Bonney, Lucius.
Bosworth, Constant D.
Coburn, Greenleaf D.
Cole, Cyrus.
Comson, Benjamin.
Crockett, Martin.
Crockett, Ephraim S.
Crockett, Solomon.
Cummings, Jesse.
Deering, James.
Drew, Walter B.
Ellis, Eleazer.
Faunce, Seth H.

Frank, Nehemiah.
Frost, Henry.
Frost, William,3d.
Foster, Nathaniel, Jr.
Gurney, Isaac P.
Gurney, John.
Hill, Benjamin.
Holt, Dudley B.
Hor, Joseph.
Hor, Nathan.
Linnell, Luther.
Lord, Nathaniel.
Lovejoy, Henry B.
Morse, Nathan, Jr.
Morgan, Jesse.

Noble, Lorenzo H.
Peabody, Benjamin, Jr.
Pike, Prescott S.
Pratt, Andrew.
Pratt, Alanson S.
Rich, Aaron W.
Richardson, Darius.
Richardson, Lyman.
Shaw, Cyrus.
Standish, Ellis, Jr.
Stevens, William.
Tarbox, Hanson.
Thayer, Ebenezer.
Witt, William P.

AROOSTOOK WAR. 63

Muster Roll of Lieutenant Hiram Pishon's Company of Riflemen in the Detachment of drafted Militia of Maine, called into actual service by the State for the protection of its Northeastern Frontie,r, from the twenty-fifth day of February, 1839, the time of its rendezvous at Augusta, Maine, to the sixteenth day of April, 1839, when discharged or mustered.

CAPTAIN. Hubbard Lovejoy.	LIEUTENANT. Hiram Pishon.	ENSIGN. Daniel Bryant.
SERGEANTS. H. S. P. Marr. David P. Lovejoy. James B. Willey. Lyman Waire.	CORPORALS. George Richardson. William H. Seaver. Joseph Grant, Jr. Samuel D. Bragg.	MUSICIANS. Llewellyn Wing. Jesse P. Bussell.
Beane, Nathan. Booker, Nicholas. Brown, Stephen D. Chandler, B. W. Durrell, Noah P. Ellis, Alonzo. Ellis, Solomon. Gage, Alexander. Gillmore, John F.	PRIVATES. Jaquith, Josiah. Johnson, Albert. Kilgore, Thomas. Lambert, Joseph. Libby, William M. Moulton, James M. Owen, Jefferson. Ramsdell, Oren A. Raymond, Ralph T.	Starbird, Levi. Smith, John O. Tebbetts, James. Wing, R. M. Wing, B. C. Weeks, R. I. Williams, William.

AROOSTOOK WAR.

Muster Roll of Captain Stillman Nash's Company of Infantry in the Detachment of drafted Militia of Maine, called into actual service by the State, for the protection of its Northeastern Frontier, from the fourth day of March, 1839, the time of its rendezvous at Calais, Maine to the sixth day of April, 1839, when discharged or mustered.

CAPTAIN.
Stillman Nash.

LIEUTENANT.
Michael Shea.

ENSIGN.
Pillsbury Stevens.

SERGEANTS.
Woodbury Leighton.
Joseph Hutchings, Jr.
Asa D. Webb.
Amaziah Fickett.

CORPORALS.
Mark L. Bunker.
Nathaneal Stover.
Major Densmore.
Otis Fickett.

MUSICIANS.
Daniel W. Dinsmore.
Uriah Merritt.

Anderson, John.
Archibald, Thomas.
Ash, Robert.
Babbidge, John.
Brown, Arthur.
Brown, Edward.
Brown, Oliver.
Bunker, Jeremiah.
Carter, Lewis.
Clemmons, William.
Coffin, Amos.
Cole, Nathaniel H.
Colson, Philo L.
Decker, Harvey.
Dickson, William.
Dorman, Wilson.
Gay, Jeremiah.
Grace, Joseph.
Guptill, Nathaniel.

PRIVATES.
Hamilton, Henry.
Joy, Hollis.
Joy, William.
Kelley, Ebenezer.
Leighton, Almon.
Leighton, John.
Leighton, Thomas.
Nash, Abner.
Nash, Levi.
Nugent, William.
Perry, Josiah W.
Perry, Ozias B.
Pinkham, Uriah.
Ray, Judson.
Robinson, John J.
Roff, Hiram.
Roff, John.
Royal, Tristram.
Sargent, Henry.

Sargent, John.
Stevens, Thomas H.
Stover, Sylvanus.
Strout, Ephraim.
Strout, George.
Strout, John.
Strout, William.
Tracey, Darius O.
Tracey, Wheeler.
Tracey, William.
Wallace, Joseph.
White, George.
White, Tilley.
Whitten, Harris.
Willey, Enoch.
Young, David.
Young, David, 2d.
Young, Jacob.
Young, Kendall.

AROOSTOOK WAR. 65

Muster Roll of Captain Joseph Perry's Company of Light Infantry in the Detachment of drafted Militia of Maine, called into actual service by the State, for the protection of its Northeastern Frontier, from the twenty-fiifth day of February, 1839, the time of its rendezvous at Augusta, Maine, to the fifteenth day of April, 1839, when mustered.

CAPTAIN.	LIEUTENANT.	ENSIGN.
Joseph Perry.	Dudley L. Haines.	Samuel Bowman.
SERGEANTS.	CORPORALS.	MUSICIANS.
Elbridge G. Towle.	James Peacock.	....
True Whittier.	George Young, Jr.	
William Lawrence, 2d.	Oliver P. Hooper.	
Josiah M. Fogg.	Harvey Ladd.	
	PRIVATES.	
Adams, Albert.	Hill, Jotham.	Norton, Russell.
Allen, Asa.	Hilman, David.	Peacock, Solomon.
Bean, Henry A.	Hodgdon, Allen.	Peacock, William.
Berry, Arthur.	Holbrook, Asa C.	Perkins, Barzillai.
Blackwell, Thomas E.	Hutchins, Silas.	Porter, Charles.
Burgess, Joseph, Jr.	Jacobs, Benjamin F.	Porter, William.
Campbell, James.	Jewell, Elias L.	Remick, Benjamin.
Cannon, Nathan.	Johnson, Sanford.	Seiders, Charles A.
Collins, Charles.	Kimball, Jacob.	Shepherd, Joseph R.
Fisk, Thomas.	Lewis, Thomas.	Smith, Taylor.
Fuller, William P.	Libby, Benjamin, Jr.	Sprague, Edmund.
Furbush, Isaac.	Longley, William M.	Stanford, Alvin.
Glass, George.	Lord, John H.	Stetson, Caleb.
Gove, Samuel M.	Lundy, Sanford P.	Taylor, James.
Gray, Cyrus H.	McCausland, William H.	Tobey, Harrison.
Gray, William.	Morgan, John.	Williams, Miles.
Heyward, Mathew.	Morse, Nathan W.	Walcott, Elmer B.
Higgins, Elisha S.	Murray, Reuben.	

5

Muster Roll of Captain Hiram A. Pollard's Company of Infantry in the Detachment of drafted Militia of Maine called into actual service by the State, for the protection of its Northeastern Frontier, from the sixth day of March 1839, the time of its rendezvous at Augusta, Maine, to the twenty-ninth day of March, 1839 when discharged or mustered.

CAPTAIN.
Hiram A. Pollard.

LIEUTENANT.
William A. Tobey.

ENSIGN.
Alonzo R. Allen.

SERGEANTS.
Alexander Dwinell.
Jasper Marston.
Lewis Jones.
Parlee Bailey.

CORPORALS.
John Haskell.
Jacob Waterman.
Hiram Bonney.
John Thompson.

MUSICIANS.
Parlin Baker.
Benjamin B. Murch.

Allen, Pliny.
Andrews, Stephen.
Benson, Samuel.
Bicknell, George.
Bradford, Daniel.
Bradford, Philemon A.
Bridgham, Sydenham.
Brown, Edward.
Bumpus, Daniel.
Chase, Daniel.
Chase, Sarson, Jr.
Chipman, Amos.
Conant, Alonzo.
Crooker, Charles.
Drake, John C.
Dudley, Benjamin.
Fales, Curtis.
Foss, William M.

PRIVATES.
Gilman, Ansel.
Gurney, Charles J.
Gurney, Samuel.
Hall, Charles.
Hall, Elisha.
Harlow, Elbridge G.
Harris, Benjamin.
Harridan, Washington F.
Hutchinson, Stephen D.
Irish, Abram M.
Leavitt, Hiram.
Linnell, Enoch.
Merrill, Charles.
Merrill, Hiram.
Merrill, Lorenzo.
Moody, Sylvanus P.
Morgan, Solomon, Jr.

Murdock, Edmund.
Nason, Jeremiah.
Packard, Noah.
Pollard, William.
Ray, Washington.
Record, Benjamin H.
Richmond, Alanson.
Richmond, Solomon.
Robinson, Alexander.
Rogers, William.
Rose, Alden.
Stetson, David.
Turner, Alexander.
Varrill, Lewis.
Whitman, Barza.
Wilson, Charles.
Winslow, Barnabas.

AROOSTOOK WAR.

Muster Roll of Captain David R. Ripley's Company of Riflemen in the Detachment of drafted Militia of Maine, called into actual service by the State for the protection of its Northeastern Frontier from the sixth day of March, 1839, the time of its rendezvous at Augusta, Maine, to the twenty-seventh day of March 1839, when discharged or mustered.

CAPTAIN.	LIEUTENANT.	ENSIGN.
David R. Ripley.	Jason Mitchell.	Charles Young, Jr.
SERGEANTS.	**CORPORALS.**	**MUSICIANS.**
Philip Mason.	Daniel H. Irish.	Henry Young.
Benjamin B. Sturtevant.	Thaddeus R. Knight.	Lemuel Knight.
Job Ryerson.	Calvin Gamage.	
Ira Smart.	Roswell Briggs.	
	PRIVATES.	
Allen, Charles H.	Jones, Simeon H.	Robinson, Francis F.
Andrews, Simeon F.	Keene, Cyrus A.	Royal, William.
Barrows, Benjamin B.	Kennison, John R.	Russell, Moses B.
Brown, Hansen.	Knight, Moses.	Skoffield, Richard T.
Buck, Spaulding.	Kildreth, Asa.	Smith, George M.
Bumpus, Luther S.	Libbey, Benjamin.	Stowell, Elias.
Caswell, Horatio.	Lombard, Simon.	Tuell, Alonzo.
Chandler, Charles Y.	Mayberry, Joshua.	Walker, Otis.
Davy, Asaph.	Merrill, Josiah.	Weston, Joseph.
Dresser, Benjamin L.	McIntire, Ephraim.	White, Joel, Jr.
Ellis, Isaac.	Norris, Alden W.	Winslow, Luther P.
Evans, Elbridge G.	Norris, Trafton.	Winship, Albert.
Foster, Luther F.	Philbrick, Lucius.	
Frank, Levi.	Rawson, Horace.	
Gazlin, Thomas.	Richardson Bemis.	
Harding, Charles.	Ring, David.	

AROOSTOOK WAR.

Muster Roll of Captain Nathaniel Sawyer's Company of Riflemen in the Detachment of drafted Militia of Maine, called into actual service by the State, for the protection of its Northeastern Frontier, from the twentieth day of February, 1839, the time of its rendezvous at Bangor, Maine, to the twenty-fourth day of April, 1839, when discharged or mustered.

CAPTAIN.
Nathaniel Sawyer.

LIEUTENANT.
Andrew D. Bean.

ENSIGN.
Charles Jones.

SERGEANTS.
John A. York.
Hiram York.
Joseph York·
Sewall Chase.

CORPORALS.
Lewis Goodwin.
Daniel Pattee.
John Goodwin.
Simeon E. Ricker.

MUSICIANS.
James Pattee.
Westerly Grindal.
George Damon.

PRIVATES.

Avery, Jeremiah.
Banks, Obadiah.
Bartlett, Joseph.
Bartlett, Thomas W.
Bedee, Richard H.
Bickford, Charles.
Brown, Josiah.
Bryant, John.
Carley, Alvin H.
Clark, William.
Copps, Moses.
Cothrill, William.
Craig, Henry.
Drake, Salmon A.
Eastman, Jacob W.
Emery, John.
Flagg, Jeremiah.
Floyd, Joshua B.

Frost, Ivory.
Garland, Carrol.
Grant, Stephen, Jr.
Hawes, Luther.
Harden, Isaac.
Higgins, Jeremiah.
Hogan, William S.
Hemmenway Joseph D.
Jameson, William.
Kelley, George A.
Kimball, Lewis.
Lancaster, Royal.
Longfellow, Newell.
Luce, Oliver.
Mason, Broadstreet, Jr.
Mason, J. A. C.
Merrill, True.
Meader, William.

Mitchell, Joseph A.
Packard, Alfred.
Porter, David.
Richardson, George.
Ricker, Samuel.
Sawyer, Daniel G.
Shirley, William.
Sidelinger, Samuel.
Smith, Alexander.
Smith, Augustus W.
Smith, Gustavus W.
Smith, Otis.
Staples, Norris.
Stephens, Nathan.
Twitchell, Asa C.
York, Rufus.
Young, Joseph D.

AROOSTOOK WAR. 69

Muster Roll of Captain Reuben S. Smart's Company of Cavalry in the Detachment of drafted Militia of Maine, called into actual service by the State, for the protection of its Northeastern Frontier, from the twenty-third day of February, 1839, the time of its rendezvous at Bangor, Maine, to the sixteenth day of April 1839, when discharged or mustered.

CAPTAIN.	LIEUTENANT.	CORNET.
Reuben S. Smart.	Bidfield Plummer.	William B. Hawes.
SERGEANTS.	CORPORALS.	MUSICIAN.
Stephen Colson, O. Sgt.	Jacob Curtis.	James N. Clements.
John G. Chase.	Elisha Persons, 2d.	
Henry S. Lackey.	Jonathan A. Carlton.	
Giles C. Grant.	Samuel F. Stinson.	
	PRIVATES.	
Carlton, Washington.	Hichborn, Nathan H.	Pomroy, Francis N.
Cole, Nathan C.	Kelley, John F.	Robinson, Charles N. B.
Curtis, Alfred.	Lambert, Jesse.	Robertson, Richard, Jr.
Curtis, George B.	Libby, John C.	Segee, George W.
Curtis, Gideon.	Mitchell, Elijah S.	Stafford, Edward B.
Curtis, John W.	Moulton, Randall.	Stearns, David, Jr.
Downs, Daniel.	Murray, Samuel.	Stinson, William B.
Durham, James.	Nealley, Daniel D.	Stubbs, Timothy.
Ellingwood, John.	Nickerson, Freeman.	Treadwell, James.
Ewell, Dodge N.	Nickerson, Nathaniel.	Trundy, Levi.
Folsom, Andrew.	Patterson, Isaac.	Tyler, James.
George, Obadiah.	Pendleton, James H.	Verrill, William.
George, Stephen D.	Perkins, Thomas.	West, Samuel.
Hall, George H.		

Muster Roll of Captain Charles H. Wing's Company of Riflemen in the Detachment of drafted Militia of Maine, called into actual service by the State for the protection of its Northeastern Frontier, from the twentieth day of Februray, 1839, the time of its rendezvous at Bangor, Maine, to the twenty-second day of April 1839, when discharged or mustered.

CAPTAIN.
Charles H. Wing.

LIEUTENANT.
Abram Morris.

ENSIGN.
Simon P. Atkins.

SERGEANTS.
Thomas C. Crehore.
William B. Walker.
Daniel B. Hall.
William H. Ginn.
J. Selden Burbank.
Micah P. Erskine.

CORPORALS.
Samuel Spencer.
Joseph L. Buck.
John G. Orcott.
Henry Balch.

MUSICIANS.
John A. Heath.
Zebah W. Burrill.

PRIVATES.

Burrill, Harvey M.
Bowes, Spencer G.
Connolly, John H.
Emery, Ambrose.
Emery, Rufus.
Emerson, Isaac D.
Farnham, John.
Fitz, Charles T.
Gray, Ephraim.
Hall, Josiah, Jr.

Holt, Stephen D.
Hopkins, Samuel M.
Hutchinson, Benjamin F.
Libbey, Charles.
Little, William, Jr.
Mason, Ethan A.
Moore, Benjamin.
Morse, Isaac W.
Noyes, George.
Perkins, Gordon.

Prim, John.
Rea, John, Jr.
Smith, Benjamin R.
Smith, Joseph B.
Snowman, John.
Staples, Joshua.
Straw, Robert C.
Stubbs, Cyrus.
Taylor, Elijah.
Thompson, Tobias.

AROOSTOOK WAR.

Muster Roll of Lieutenant Israel W. Woodward's Company of Infantry in the Detachment of drafted Militia of Maine, called into actual service by the State, for the protection of its Northeastern Frontier, from the twenty-fifth day of February, 1839, the time of its rendezvous at Augusta, Maine, to the fifteenth day of April, 1839, when mustered.

LIEUTENANT.	LIEUTENANT.	ENSIGN.
Israel W. Woodward.	Samuel E. Bean.	Charles P. Craig.

SERGEANTS.	CORPORALS.	
John Warren.	Julius Burke.	
Ebenezer Toothaker.	Joseph Robie.	
Joseph Grover.	Lewis Card.	
Benjamin Potter.	Ivory W. Coombs.	

	PRIVATES.	
Bailey Lewis.	Howes, Edward.	Pierce, Jonathan W.
Dill, John A.	Jaquith, John.	Pinkham, Charles.
Douglass, Robert H.	McCausland, Charles.	Pinkham, Reuben, Jr.
Douglass, William.	Merrill, Ebenezer.	Reed, Thomas.
Fisher, Luther.	Neal, Daniel.	Stoddard, Christopher.
Hanscomb, Joseph.	Nutting, Asa.	Stuart, Amos C.
Hamlin, Jesse.	Paine, James.	Tibbetts, Andrew.

Errata.

Page 26. Read Lynn, David, instead of Lyon, David.
Page 29. Read Ephraim instead of Ephram.
Page 30. Read Isaiah instead of Isiah, and Ephraim instead of Ephriam.
Page 32. Read Gershom instead of Greshom.
Page 33. Read Ephraim instead of Ephram.
Page 41. Read Cummings instead of Cumming.
Page 43. Read Othniel instead of Othuiel, and promoted after words prefixed by star.
Page 45. Read Daniel instead of Daniei.
Page 48. Read Barzillai instead of Barzillia.

INDEX OF NAMES OF MEN IN THE AROOSTOOK WAR, 1839.

A

Name	Page
Abbot, Aaron J.	31
Abbott, Freeman F.	52
Abbott, Horatio N.	47
Abbot, John, Sergt.	59
Abbot, Levi G.	55
Abbott, Philip, Corpl.	51
Abbot, Samuel.	61
Abbot, Thomas.	41
Abbot, Willard.	41
Abbott, Willard.	57
Abbott, Moses.	37
Abbott, William W.	52
Adams, Albert.	65
Adams, Benj., Ens.	49
Adams, James.	61
Adams, James W.	58
Adams, John M., Sergt.	47
Adams, William.	61
Additon, Charles A.	28
Akers, William J.	31
Alden, Amasa, Mus'n.	51
Alden, Benj., Jr.	45
Alden, Columbus.	45
Alden, Loren.	45
Aldrich, Asa L.	34
Allen, Asa.	65
Allen, Alonzo R., Ens.	66
Allen, Charles H.	67
Allen, Daniel F., Ens.	55
Allen, Daniel F., Sergt.	55
Allen, David.	38
Allen, George.	27
Allen, Isaac N.	55
Allen, Joseph S.	29
Allen, Joseph.	53
Allen, Josiah.	27
Allen, Pliny.	66
Allen, Samuel.	35
Allen, Stephen W.	37
Alley, Hiram.	34
Ames, Almarin.	41
Ames, Amariah W.	48
Ames, John.	60
Ames, John, Mus'n.	46
Anderson, John.	64
Andrews, Ephraim K., Sergt.	31
Andrews, Charles, Lieut. Col.	22
Andrews, James.	47
Andrews, Robert R.	53
Andrews, Simeon F.	67
Andrews, Stephen.	66
Andrews, Thaddeus B.	52
Andrews, William.	47
Annis, George W.	56
Annis, John G.	38
Annis, Joseph S.	48
Anthony, Joseph, Capt.	26
Appleton, William.	48
Archibald, Thomas.	64
Armstrong, Geo. W., Sergt.	27
Arno, Hiram.	49
Arno, John.	45
Arnold, Albion P., Capt.	27
Arnold, Lemuel.	57
Ash, Robert.	64
Ashley, Frederic.	34
Atkins, Simon P., Ens.	70
Atwood, George M.	27
Atwood, William E., Lieut.	35
Austin, George, Mus'n.	28
Austin, Hezekiah.	31
Austin, James.	42
Austin, Jesse.	50
Austin, William B., Lieut.	33
Avery, Jeremiah.	68
Averill, William, Ord. Sergt.	60
Ayers, Bradbury B.	59
Ayer, Daniel F., Corp'l.	27

B

Name	Page
Babb, Joseph H.	30
Babb, Libbeus H.	39
Babbidge, John.	64
Babcock, John W.	61
Bachelder, William.	41
Bacon, Francis.	34
Bacon, Samuel F.	30
Bagley, James.	29
Bagley, Levi.	60
Bailey, Daniel.	48
Bailey, Daniel.	59
Bailey, Henry, Capt.	29
Bailey, John H.	30
Bailey, Lewis.	71
Bailey, Moody.	58
Bailey, Parlee, Sergt.	66
Bailey, Philip.	59
Bailey, William.	47
Baker, Edward D.	35

	Page		Page
Baker, Forbes	33	Bean, Andrew D., Lieut	68
Baker, Jeremy, Corpl	60	Bean, Carlos	35
Baker, Luke, Jr	52	Bean, Daniel	48
Baker, Parlin, Mus'n	66	Bean, Dudley D., Corpl	60
Baker, Samuel	35	Bean, Dudley, Jr., Sergt	39
Balch, Henry, Corpl	70	Bean, Henry A	65
Ballard, William, Jr	41	Bean, George	31
Bancroft, Daniel M	62	Bean, George T	30
Bangs, Samuel S	30	Bean, John H	36
Banks, Daniel	38	Bean, Josiah	31
Banks, David P	32	Bean, Samuel E., Lieut	71
Banks, Horace, Sergt	59	Bean, Samuel G., Fife Maj	24
Banks, Obadiah	68	Bean, Sylvanus B., Sergt	45
Banks, Orrin	55	Bean, Vear	31
Barbour, Levi	38	Beane, Nathan	63
Barbour, Seward P	30	Beane, William	34
Barbrick, Moses	31	Beattie, Patterson	31
Barden, Oren	35	Bedee, Isaac	57
Barden, Othniel	57	Bedee, Richard H	68
Barker, Abram A., Ens	39	Beedle, William	50
Barker, Elden, Lieut	24	Bell, John, 3d	52
Barker, Jonathan	53	Bennett, Alanson	54
Barker, Joseph	31	Bennett, Andrew	45
Barker, Nathan, Capt	30	Bennett, Gilman	31
Barker, Waterman	31	Bennett, John, Jr	56
Barnard, Charles, Sgt. Maj	24	Benson, James S	62
Barnard, John D., Capt	31	Benson, Samuel	66
Barney, William	48	Benson, Thomas J	56
Barrows, Benjamin B	67	Berry, Albert G., Corpl	34
Barrows, Joseph, Adjt	22	Berry, Arthur	65
Barrows, Samuel	61	Berry, David	57
Barrett, Horatio, Lieut	59	Berry, Isaac	53
Barstow, Hetherty	53	Berry, Jonathan S., Corpl	51
Bartlett, Cyrus	42	Berry, Mial	56
Bartlett, David	34	Besse, Joshua	31
Bartlett, Frederick K., Capt	40	Bessey, Alexander H	44
Bartlett, Jonathan A	47	Bessey, Jonathan B	49
Bartlett, Joseph	51	Bickford, Almond	42
Bartlett, Joseph	68	Bickford, Charles	68
Bartlett, Joseph, Sergt	58	Bickford, Enoch W	59
Bartlett, Nehemiah	61	Bickford, Joseph H	42
Bartlett, Ruel, Corpl	46	Bicknell, George	66
Bartlett, Thomas W	68	Billings, David L	41
Bartlett, William, Corpl	31	Billings, Dexter	38
Bartlett, Zenas	58	Billings, John D	52
Bassett, James	52	Bird, Samuel, Ens	31
Bassick, Samuel	37	Bisbee, Charles	52
Batchelder, Daniel	61	Bisbee, Solomon, Sergt	52
Batchelder, David, 2d	36	Bishop, Joseph S., Capt	24
Batchelder, Dodge	58	Bishop, William H	36
Batchelder, Geo. W., Brig. Gen.	22	Bishop, Zadoc	28
Batchelder, James	58	Bither, Dennis J., Mus'n	61
Batchelder, John, 2d	58	Bither, Ira	35
Batchelder, Phineas, Sergt	40	Blackwell, Sylvanus	44
Batchelder, Royal H., Mus'n	58	Blackwell, Thomas E	65
Batchelder, William	54	Blagdon, Samuel	35
Bates, Charles B., Lieut	27	Blaisdell, Orrin W	27
Bates, George, Chaplain	22	Blake, Caleb	45
Bates, William C., Sergt	49	Blake, Charles	38
Bazzell, William F	59	Blake, Daniel P	55
Beals, Benj., Capt	28	Blake, Dudley	26
Beals, Hiram	45	Blake, Joseph, Corpl	36
Beals, Isaiah, Lieut	57	Blake, Levi	35
Beals, Samuel	48	Blake, Wade	42
Beale, Seth, Jr., 2d Lieut	45	Blanchard, Charles, Chaplain	22
Beal, William D	29	Blodget, Hiram	37

INDEX. 75

	Page		Page
Blodgett, Horace	44	Brown, Benj., Jr	57
Blunt, Enoch M	60	Brown, Cyrus, Mus'n	36
Bodfish, Albert G., Paymaster	22	Brown, David G	57
Bodwell, David	26	Brown, Edward	64
Bolton, Benj., Jr., Sergt	37	Brown, Edward	66
Bond, John	30	Brown, Francis D	52
Bond, John B., Corpl	41	Brown, Hansen	67
Bonney, Hiram, Corpl	66	Brown, James	34
Bonney, Lucius	62	Brown, James	53
Boobar, Calvin I	54	Brown, John A., Lieut	29
Boobier, Rufus	39	Brown, John W	27
Booker, James	50	Brown, John	31
Booker, Nicholas	63	Brown, John	40
Booker, Washington	31	Brown, Joseph	31
Boothby, Benj., Sergt	30	Brown, Josiah	40
Boston, Gershom	32	Brown, Josiah	68
Boston, John T	39	Brown, Oliver	64
Bosworth, Constant D	62	Brown, Perkins	40
Bosworth, William, Jr	57	Brown, Reuben P., Sergt	51
Bourne, Jason L., Corpl	61	Brown, Reuben	57
Bowden, John	46	Brown, Samuel, Jr., Corpl	52
Bowden, Sylvester	54	Brown, S. V. R. G., Corpl	30
Bowes, Spencer G	70	Brown, Simon	39
Bowker, Cyprian	38	Brown, Stephen D	63
Bowman, David C. B	22	Brown, Wm. McE., Sergt	43
Bowman, Samuel, Ens	65	Brown, Wm. McE	57
Boyd, John	41	Brown, William	59
Boynton, David, 2d, Sergt	36	Bryant, Epaphrus R., Sergt	26
Boynton, James S	47	Bryant, Daniel, Ens	63
Boynton, James M	49	Bryant, John	68
Boynton, Nathaniel, Corpl	54	Bryant, Otis	46
Brackett, Dexter W	38	Bryant, Walter L., Mus'n	52
Brackett, Simeon	47	Bucks, Ira B	48
Bracey, William	33	Buck, John W	59
Bradeen, Isaac	51	Buck, Joseph L., Corpl	70
Bradbury, Jabez, Lieut	24	Buck, Spaulding	67
Bradbury, John, Corpl	32	Buckley, Franklin	34
Bradbury, Reuben	32	Buckmore, Chas. W., Corpl	37
Bradford, Daniel	66	Buckman, Samuel	30
Bradbury, Jesse, Lieut	45	Budson, Joseph, Sergt	41
Bradford, Philemon A	66	Budge, John N	35
Bradley, Thomas	48	Bullard, Asa	30
Bragdon, Elbridge H., Sergt	48	Buffam, Charles	60
Bragdon, Nathaniel	30	Bumpus, Daniel	66
Bragdon, Seth L	30	Bumpus, Luther S	67
Bragdon, Thomas	56	Bunker, Benj. J	34
Bragg, James	40	Bunker, Benj	54
Bragg, Samuel D., Corpl	63	Bunker, Jeremiah	64
Branch, Adrastus	32	Bunker, Mark L., Corpl	64
Branch, Wm. D., Corpl	42	Bunker, Rufus	50
Bray, Ebenezer	45	Bunker, Sewall	34
Bray, Joseph, Corpl	41	Bunker, Silas, Jr	35
Brickett, James, Corpl	52	Burbank, J. Selden, Sergt	70
Bridge, Levi, Jr	57	Burgess, Joseph, Jr	65
Bridge, Samuel	58	Burgess, Thomas A	48
Bridgham, Sydenham	66	Burleigh, James P	57
Brier, Robert, Jr	37	Burleigh, Walter	32
Briggs, Alanson, Sergt	38	Burke, Julius, Corpl	71
Briggs, Daniel H	45	Burnham, Hiram, Capt	33
Briggs, John	26	Burnham, Jeremiah, Ens	40
Briggs, Roswell, Corpl	67	Burnham, Mark	58
Brooks, Chas. B., Corpl	56	Burnham, Royal R	40
Brooks, Daniel	48	Burnham, Wm. W., Corpl	48
Brooks, Joseph	37	Burns, George	41
Brown, Abial	50	Burrell, Samuel, Capt	32
Brown, Arthur	64	Burrill, Harvey M	70

Name	Page	Name	Page
Burrill, Zebah W., Mus'n	70	Chandler, Harlow	42
Burrill, Ziba	61	Chandler, Thomas	42
Burton, David	54	Chaplin, Charles E	60
Burton, Timothy	41	Chapman, Benj. P.	36
Busseil, Jesse P., Mus'n	63	Chapman, Garey	41
Butler, Ansel	34	Chapman, William I	41
Butler, Ambrose	34	Charles, Farnham	39
Butler, Jairus	36	Chase, Alexander H	58
Butler, Nathaniel R	34	Chase, Alfred, Corpl	38
Butler, Samuel	27	Chase, Daniel	66
Butters, Sewall	52	Chase, Dudley	31
Butterfield, Edmund, Sergt	56	Chase, Elbridge	51
Butterfield, Orrin	40	Chase, Eleazer	38
Buzzell, Isaac	41	Chase, Hiram	37
Buzzell, Jonathan	40	Chase, John	48
Byram, Erastus B	61	Chase, John G., Sergt	69
Byram, Orville	45	Chase, Joseph C	48
		Chase, Robert P., Mus'n	41
C		Chase, Samuel G	53
Caldwell, Wm. P., Corpl	27	Chase, Sarson, Jr	66
Caler, John B	29	Chase, Sewall, Sergt	68
Calef, Daniel	37	Chase, Stephen D	56
Calighan, Humphrey	29	Chipman, Amos	66
Campbell, Ambrose, Mus'n	33	Chipman, Hiram	55
Campbell, James, Mus'n	33	Choate, James R	27
Campbell, James	65	Christopher, William	50
Campbell, James M	33	Church, Charles	32
Campbell, Robert F., Corpl	33	Church, George W	29
Campbell, Rufus	27	Church, John, Sergt	29
Campbell, Samuel	33	Churchill, James	38
Cannon, Nathan	65	Churchill, Matthew	53
Capers, Nathaniel	48	Cilley, Benj., Corpl	54
Card, Lewis, Corpl	71	Clark, Abram	44
Card, Thornton	48	Clark, Albin B., Ens	57
Carlisle, George W	54	Clark, Amos, Jr	28
Carleton, James Henry, Lieut	61	Clark, Charles M	55
Carlton, Jonathan A., Corpl	69	Clark, Daniel W., Capt	34
Carlton, Washington	69	Clark, Daniel, Mus'n	52
Carley, Alvin H	68	Clark, Ensign	34
Carpenter, George S., Brig. Maj.	22	Clark, Gustavus, Lieut	24
Carpenter, Joshua, Act. Brig. Maj	22	Clark, Gustavus, Lieut	42
Carr, Justus S	41	Clark, Hezekiah C	38
Carter, Amos	56	Clark, James, Capt	35
Carter, Henry L., Corpl	26	Clark, James, Jr	28
Carter, Jonathan	48	Clark, John M	34
Carter, Lewis	64	Clark, John M	30
Carver, Caleb	28	Clark, Jonathan, Sergt	38
Carver, James	48	Clark, Robert H	49
Cary, Thomas, Corpl	45	Clark, Samuel	40
Caswell, Chandler	28	Clark, Sherburn W	59
Caswell, Horatio	67	Clark, William H., Sergt	26
Caswell, John A	56	Clark, William	68
Caswell, Justus	56	Claridge, Hiram S., Corpl	40
Caswell, Marcus	28	Clemmons, William	64
Cayton, James	37	Clements, James N., Mus'n	69
Chadbourne, Benj	40	Cleaveland, James B., Lieut	24
Chadbourne, John W	39	Cleveland, James B	60
Chadbourne, Josiah	49	Clifford, Isaac B	32
Chadman, John O	35	Clock, Abram	44
Chaffin, George G	56	Clough, Benj., Sergt	49
Chamberlain, Walker, Sergt	42	Clough, George W	36
Champion, John	40	Clough, Noah	61
Chandler, Barnabas S	29	Clough, Jacob	42
Chandler, B. W	63	Coats, Thomas G	34
Chandler, Charles F	30	Cobb, John	53
Chandler, Charles Y	67	Cobb, Reuben S	53

INDEX. 77

Name	Page
Cobb, Stephen	53
Coburn, Frederick, Jr.	45
Coburn, Greenfield D.	62
Coburn, Jonas	58
Codman, Randolph A. L., Lieut.	55
Coffin, Amos	64
Coffin, Daniel	52
Coffin, Isaiah	30
Coffin, James, Jr.	28
Coffin, Jonathan C.	31
Coffin, John W., Sergt.	33
Coffin, Samuel F.	31
Cofran, Franklin	37
Cogan, William E. D.	26
Cole, Cyrus	62
Cole, Ira	39
Cole, John	57
Cole, Nathan C.	69
Cole, Nathaniel H.	64
Cole, Sumner	36
Cole, Sylvanus	39
Colburn, Jarathaneal	38
Collier, F. M., Sergt.	50
Collins, Charles	65
Collins, Ebenezer, Jr.	55
Collins, William H.	50
Colomy, Abraham, Corpl.	61
Colson, Jonas	34
Colson, Philo L.	64
Colson, Samuel, Jr.	33
Colson, Stephen, Ord. Sergt.	69
Colson, Theophilus, 2d	37
Comery, Sandford	61
Comson, Benjamin	62
Comstock, Solomon	59
Conant, Alonzo	66
Condon, Daniel	54
Connor, Chas. H., Ord. Sergt.	43
Conners, John	33
Conners, Samuel	33
Connery, John	29
Connolly, John H.	70
Cony, Robert A., Surgeon	22
Cook, Hezekiah	46
Cook, John	46
Cook, Eli	43
Cookson, John	40
Cookson, Reuben	60
Cook, Seth F.	60
Cook, Timothy M., Sergt.	35
Cooley, Horace S.	26
Coolidge, Silas	34
Coombs, Albert	59
Coombs, Ivory W., Corpl.	71
Coombs, James W.	37
Cooper, James	59
Copeland, Gardner	57
Copps, Moses	68
Corliss, William	35
Cornforth, Charles, Ens.	32
Corson, Benjamin F.	32
Corson, Eben S.	32
Corson, Erastus	40
Corson, Frederick F.	55
Costelow, Samuel W.	61
Cothrill, William	68
Cottle, Samuel F.	40
Cotton, Horace	54
Cotton, William	29
Cousins, Joseph N.	46
Cousins, William	61
Covell, John	50
Cowan, Levi, Jr.	49
Cowan, John, Jr.	60
Craig, Charles P., Ens.	71
Craig, Henry	68
Crane, Reuben, 2d., Capt.	36
Creamer, Gardner	46
Crehore, Thomas C., Sergt.	70
Cripps, Josiah	46
Crocker, Freeman	48
Crocker, Henry	48
Crocker, John	56
Crocker, Moses	48
Crocker, Samuel	50
Crockett, Ephraim S.	62
Crockett, John, Jr.	51
Crockett, Lathrop L., Sergt.	55
Crockett, Martin	62
Crockett, Solomon	62
Crooker, Charles	66
Cross, Joseph	37
Cross, Joseph K.	61
Cross, William	35
Crowell, James	57
Crowley, Nathaniel	29
Cummings, Amos	29
Cummings, Francis I., Lieut.	41
Cummings, Francis J., Adjt.	43
Cummings, Geo. W., Lieut. Col.	22
Cummings, Goodridge, Ens.	59
Cummings, Henry, Mus'n.	52
Cummings, Jesse A.	28
Cummings, Jesse	62
Cummings, John L., Corpl.	52
Cummings, Moses C.	50
Cummings, Samuel B.	29
Cummings, William B.	29
Cumston, Robert M.	40
Cunningham, Anson	46
Cunningham, James	37
Cunningham, James	37
Cunningham, James	37
Cunningham, Thomas	41
Cunningham, William	37
Curtis, Alfred	69
Curtis, Calvin B.	33
Curtis, Ezra	54
Curtis, George B.	69
Curtis, Gideon	69
Curtis, Jacob, Corpl.	69
Curtis, John W.	69
Curtis, Paul	46
Curtis, Rufus G.	60
Curtis, Theo. L., Corpl.	53
Curtis, Uzziel	46
Cushman, Alden	45
Cushman, Ellis	57
Cushman, Horace, Mus'n.	45
Cushman, Jonathan	45
Cushman, Joseph	35
Cushman, Nelson, Corpl.	45
Cutler, Lysander, Lieut. Col.	22

AROOSTOOK WAR.

D

Name	Page
Daggett, Ebenezer	40
Daggett, John	45
Dam, Joel F	59
Dam, Leader N	59
Dammon, Ezekiel	38
Damon, George, Mus'n	68
Damon, Joseph B	60
Damren, Chandler	59
Damren, Joel T	42
Daniels, George D	37
Daniels, James M	40
Daniels, Joseph	45
Dane, Francis B	36
Dane, Solomon S	36
Darling, Walker, Corpl	59
Davice, John C	30
Davidson, George	39
Davidson, John	56
Davies, Edward H	55
Davis, Asa, 2d	60
Davis, Asahel	59
Davis, Andrew S	58
Davis, Charles, Corpl	59
Davis, David B	59
Davis, Eliphalet	38
Davis, Elisha	61
Davis, James P	61
Davis, James M	61
Davis, John P., Sergt	41
Davis, Jonas W., Mus'n	55
Davis, Moses	50
Davis, Robert P	58
Davis, Samuel B	36
Davis, Sylvanus G	52
Davis, William	32
Davy, Asaph	67
Day, Andrew N	57
Day, Charles	37
Day, Edmond	34
Day, Samuel B	28
Day, Thomas	52
Day, William, Corpl	28
Dearbon, John W., Corpl	47
Dearborn, Joseph, Sergt	62
Decker, Harvey	64
DeCoster, Thomas	56
Deering, James	62
Deering, Samuel	41
Delanoe, Charles G	51
Delano, Daniel, Fife Maj	24
Deling, James	59
Deluce, Joseph H	57
Dendico, Sewall	46
Dennis, Carlisle, Sergt	59
Dennis, E. E., Corpl	26
Densmore, David	57
Densmore, David	43
Densmore, Major, Corpl	64
Dennett, Mark	45
Devo, William	59
Dexter, Isaac	48
Dickinson, James	41
Dickson, William	64
Dike, William	51
Dill, John A	71
Dillingham, Benjamin	60
Dillingham, Charles E	32
Dillingham, Eben H	38
Dinsmore, Daniel W., Mus'n	64
Doble, Charles, Corpl	58
Doble, Orren	58
Doble, Phineas, Corpl	62
Doble, William, Ens	56
Dockham, Stephen B., Sergt	58
Dodge, Amazias, Mus'n	35
Dodge, Sabbina	54
Doe, Benjamin W., Sergt	55
Doe, Nahalie	59
Dolby, George	47
Donnell, Francis	30
Door, John E	54
Dority, Daniel, Capt	37
Dorman, Ephraim P	33
Dorman, Wilson	64
Dorr, Barzillai	40
Dorr, Ephraim	41
Dorr, John F	29
Dorr, Joseph P	29
Dorr, Leonard W	29
Dorr, Moses W	29
Dorr, Richard B	29
Dougherty, Truxton, Capt	24
Douglass, Israel	40
Douglass, James	54
Douglass, Robert H	71
Douglass, William	71
Dow, David, Capt	24
Dow, Stephen	48
Downs, Daniel	39
Downs, Daniel	69
Downe, Henry A	58
Downing, James W., Sergt	39
Downing, Moses	45
Drake, John C	66
Drake Salmon A	68
Draper, Hiram	58
Draper, Richard	53
Dresser, Benjamin L	67
Drew, Liberty, Sergt	58
Drew, Lorraine I	61
Drew, Seth, Sergt	57
Drew, Walter B	62
Dudley, Benjamin	66
Dudley, John S	36
Dudley, Moses S	36
Dudley Stephen	27
Dudley, William K	36
Dugan, Merrill	36
Dunbar, Alfred	33
Dunbar, John B	33
Dunham, John, Jr	41
Dunham, Othniel	43
Dunham, Sampson, Capt	38
Dunlap, Elbridge	45
Dunn, David T	28
Dunning, Valentine	35
Dunning, James, Ens	40
Dunton, Jason	61
Durham, Albert	37
Durham, James	69
Duran, Benjamin	30

INDEX. 79

Name	Page
Duran, Joseph	41
Durrell, Noah P.	63
Dwelley, Wm., Jr.	41
Dwinell, Alexander, Sergt.	66
Dyer, Alfred	30
Dyer, Asa.	34
Dyer, Benjamin	35
Dyer, Daniel Y.	45
Dyer, Emery	33
Dyer, George W.	30
Dyer, Joel	34
Dyer, Selden	42
Dyer, Simon A., Sergt.	30
Dyer, Thompson, Sergt.	43
Dyer, Thompson	57
Dyle, Edmund	44

E

Name	Page
Earle, Joseph	27
Eastman, Benjamin	59
Eastman, Jacob W.	68
Eaton, Ebenezer	56
Eaton, John C.	37
Eaton, Joseph, Ens.	37
Eaton, Nathaniel D.	35
Eaton, Sylvanus, Sergt.	54
Eddy, George W.	35
Edgerly, Daniel W.	59
Edmands, Benjamin, J.	31
Edwards, James M.	56
Edwards, John	37
Eells, Samuel F., Sergt.	48
Elder, Josiah L., Capt.	39
Elder, William S.	52
Eldridge, I. S., Sergt.	43
Eldridge, James S., Sergt.	41
Elkins, Edward N.	31
Elkins, John, Jr.	59
Ellingwood, John.	69
Elliott, Abner H.	47
Elliot, Rufus S.	58
Ellis, Alonzo.	63
Ellis, Eleazer	62
Ellis, Freeman	42
Ellis, Isaac	67
Ellis, Lemuel, Prin. Mus'n.	24
Ellis, Martin, Jr., Corpl.	47
Ellis, Nathan, Jr., Capt.	40
Ellis, Solomon	63
Emery, Ambrose	70
Emery, Amos	31
Emery, Briggs H., 2d	32
Emery, Hiram W.	46
Emery, John	68
Emery, John B.	59
Emery, John J., Lieut.	32
Emery, John S., Mus'n.	34
Emery, John W.	55
Emery, Joshua T.	30
Emery, Rufus	70
Emerson, Benjamin	61
Emerson, Benjamin D.	50
Emerson, Calvin	37
Emerson, Charles	59
Emerson, Emery	53
Emerson, Gilbert, Ens.	41
Emerson, Isaac D.	70
Emerson, John N., Sergt.	35
Emerson, Joshua L.	37
Emerson, Josiah H., Mus'n.	37
Emerson, Joseph	59
Emerson, Levi, Sergt.	43
Emerson, Levi	57
Emerson, Micah C., Corpl.	58
Emerson, William	59
Emerton, Amasa S.	41
Erskine, Micah P., Sergt.	70
Erskine, Samuel D.	24
Evans, Elbridge G.	67
Evans, James	52
Evans, John	32
Everett, Charles H.	33
Eveleth, Elisha M.	41
Eveleth, Halsey H.	55
Ewell, Dodge N.	69

F

Name	Page
Fairbanks, Cyrus C., Corpl.	27
Fairbanks, John, Maj. or Arty.	24
Fairbanks, Sylvanus, Sergt.	27
Fales, Curtis.	66
Farnham, David H.	56
Farnham, John.	70
Farnham, Joseph A.	51
Farnham, Levi O., Sergt.	43
Farnham, Levi O.	48
Farnsworth, George.	29
Farr, Converse.	55
Farr, James.	29
Farrington, Ebenezer.	61
Farrington, Moses C.	39
Farrington, Samuel.	36
Farrington, Stillman.	39
Faunce, Seth H.	62
Fellows, Nathaniel, Mus'n.	59
Fellows, Moses.	36
Felton, Jonathan W.	45
Ferguson, Nathan.	53
Ferguson, Oliver.	40
Fernald, Samuel R.	30
Ferren, Chester.	41
Fickett, Amaziah, Sergt.	64
Fickett, Otis, Corpl.	64
Field, Amos, Jr.	30
Field, Joseph, Ensign.	38
Field, Thomas, Sergt.	26
Fifield, Daniel E., Corpl.	58
Fifield, Thomas B.	58
Fish, Nathaniel B.	48
Fish, Samuel L., Capt.	41
Fish, Samuel L., Capt.	43
Fish, Sanford.	45
Fish, Stephen.	57
Fisher, Luther.	71
Fisk, Alden B.	45
Fisk, Thomas.	65
Fitts, Andrew G.	40
Fitz, Charles T.	70
Fitzgerild, Henry C.	53
Flagg, Jeremiah.	68
Flanders, Reuben, Sergt.	57

	Page		Page
Fletcher, Joseph H	26	Frost, Oliver, Aid	22
Flint, Amos, Sergt	52	Frost, Sumner, Ens	52
Flood, Jesse, Lieut	46	Frost, William, Lieut	43
Flood, Thomas N	46	Frost, William P	47
Floyd, Jeremiah	46	Frost, William P., Sergt. Major	22
Floyd, Joshua B	68	Frost, William, 3d	62
Fogg, Alvan	49	Frye, John	30
Fogg, Elliot Y., Mus'n	55	Furbush, Isaac	65
Fogg, Ezekiel F	51	Fuller, Alonzo	38
Fogg, Francis A	27	Fuller, Albion P	51
Fogg, Greenlief M., Corpl	60	Fuller, Charles P	56
Fogg, Hiram, Sergt	61	Fuller, Samuel, Jr	51
Fogg, Isaac, Mus'n	54	Fuller, William P	65
Fogg, John H	54	Fullerton, George W	40
Fogg, John M	60	Fulsom, John	39
Fogg, Josiah M., Sergt	65		
Fogg, Joseph	32	**G**	
Fogg, Peleg	40	Gage, Alexander	63
Fogg, Seth, Corpl	49	Gage, Richard	55
Fogg, William L	54	Gammon, William	56
Follett, John E	27	Gamage, Calvin, Corpl	67
Folsom, Andrew	69	Gardner, John, Capt	44
Folsom, Cyrus H	27	Gardner, William, Sergt	32
Forbes, Charles H., Corpl	41	Garland, Carrol	68
Ford, Benjamin F	56	Garland, David	46
Ford, Moses	54	Garland, Ebenezer	54
Forster, William	29	Garland, John	30
Foss, Daniel, Ens	28	Garland, John	46
Foss, John E	35	Garmon, Wilmath S., Jr	31
Foss, Levi	28	Gates, Zaloch	58
Foss, Thomas	34	Gay, Jeremiah	64
Foss, Walter	44	Gazlin, Benjamin	26
Foss, William M	66	Gazlin, Thomas	67
Foster, Charles S	44	George, George W	28
Foster, Edmund W	52	George, Obadiah	69
Foster, Ezekiel, Major Gen	22	George, Samuel T	37
Foster, Hiram	56	George, Stephen D	69
Foster, Jeremiah, Corpl	62	Geral, Daniel	40
Foster, Luther F	67	Getchell, David, Sergt	60
Foster, Nathaniel, Jr	62	Getchell, Owen, Sergt	42
Fowles, Asa	61	Gerrish, Nathaniel	54
Fowles, Daniel	41	Gerrish, Stephen S	43
Fox, Daniel, Jr	55	Gerry, Ebenezer O	48
Fox, Edmund	39	Gibbs, Franklin	57
Francis, Joseph	60	Gibbs, Heman, Jr	32
France, Sylvanus B	38	Gibbs, William H., Ens	60
Frank, James, Jr., Mus'n	53	Gibson, Parker	53
Frank, Levi	67	Gibson, Zachariah, Capt	45
Frank, Nehemiah	62	Gilbert, Gustavus, Corpl	28
Frazier, John	46	Gilbert, John N	28
Frazier, Isaac, Jr., Sergt	46	Gilbert, Judson	28
Frazier, Samuel	46	Gilbert, William H	55
Freeman, Daniel, Jr	55	Gilcrease, Hiram	31
Freeman, George	33	Giles, Benjamin	46
French, David	35	Giles, Ebenezer	33
French, George	36	Gile, Samuel H	36
French, Gideon	51	Gilley, Isaac F	26
French, Lewis R	61	Gilley, William	34
French, Washington, Ens	62	Gilman, Ansel	66
French, William R	47	Gilman, Eben	53
Frost, Alden B	51	Gilman, Enoch W	54
Frost, Enoch	54	Gilman, Samuel S., Mus'n	36
Frost, Henry	62	Gilman, John	39
Frost, Ivory	68	Gilman, Joseph, Div. Q. M	22
Frost, Moses, Surg. Mate	22	Gillmore, James H	41
Frost, Nathaniel, Capt	42	Gillmore, John F	63

INDEX. 81

Name	Page
Gilpatrick, Ignatius	34
Ginn, Caleb	43
Ginn, Wm. H., Sergt	70
Glass, George	65
Gleason, David R., Lieut	31
Gleason, Dennis	58
Glidden, Ephraim	60
Glidden, Hiram	35
Glidden, John	40
Glines, Albert G., Mus'n	47
Glines, Daniel G	31
Goddard, Edward	53
Godding, Tristram C., Sergt	58
Godfrey, Adam	26
Godfrey, David	33
Godwin, Hiram F	58
Goodwin, Francis	35
Goodwin, Enoch P	58
Goodwin, John, Corpl	68
Goodwin, Lewis, Corpl	68
Googins, Asa, Sergt	34
Googins, Rufus B	43
Googins, Thomas	34
Goold, John F	55
Gordon, Ebenezer H	40
Gordon, John	48
Gordon, Joseph M	34
Gordon, Joseph	61
Gordon, Paul S	34
Gore, John	53
Gorton, James	61
Gorton, John	61
Goss, Watson R	61
Gossom, William	45
Gott, James	34
Gould, George, Sergt	28
Gould, Isaac	48
Gould, Horace I., Corpl	40
Gould, Joseph	28
Gould, Joseph	57
Gould, Thomas	60
Gould, Thomas F	58
Gove, Elbridge G	55
Gove, Jonathan	49
Gove, Samuel M	65
Gowell, George, Corpl	55
Gowell, Hiram	55
Gowell, John	42
Gowell, John, Jr	42
Gower, Henry E	30
Grace, Joseph	64
Graffam, C. P	50
Grant, Arthur L	35
Grant, Ephraim	29
Grant, Giles C., Sergt	69
Grant, Isaac W	62
Grant, James D	29
Grant, Joseph, Jr., Corpl	63
Grant, Stephen, Jr	68
Grant, Unite	53
Graves, Sewall H	44
Gray, Alexander	54
Gray, Credepher, Corpl	37
Gray, Cyrus H	65
Gray, Ephraim	70
Gray, John	52
Gray, Judson	37
Gray, Robert	52
Gray, Samuel	50
Gray, Shadrach	41
Gray, William C	49
Gray, William	65
Green, Asa	54
Green, Charles M	30
Green, Jonas	46
Greene, George W	53
Greene, Harrison B	36
Greene, Isaac, Capt	46
Greene, John A	52
Greene, Rufus	53
Greene, Sumner	26
Greene, William	32
Greene, William	52
Greenleaf, James S., Mus'n	62
Greeley, Asa, Jr., Corpl	55
Greeley, George	37
Gribbin, Peter R	40
Griffin, Edward	36
Griffin, Leonard, Mus'n	28
Griffin, Peroz I., Corpl	53
Grindell, David R. W	57
Grindle, Ezra	37
Grindle, Ichabod, Sergt	37
Grindel, John	41
Grindle, Joseph	61
Grindle, Reuben, Jr	37
Grindle, Robert	37
Grindle, Simeon B	61
Grindal, Westerly, Mus'n	68
Gross, John	54
Gross, Joseph	54
Gross, William, Jr	51
Grover, Abraham	35
Grover, Almon	31
Grover, John, Surgeon	22
Grover, John	28
Grover, John	49
Grover, Joseph, Sergt	71
Groves, Henry	49
Grueby, Edward L	55
Gulliver, Benjamin	37
Gulliver, Thomas	60
Guptil, Benjamin	61
Guptill, Lemuel	33
Guptill, Nathaniel	64
Guptill, William	54
Guppy, William P	41
Guild, Samuel	26
Gurney, Charles J	66
Gurney, Isaac P	62
Gurney, John	62
Gurney, Samuel	66

H

Name	Page
Hackett, Amos	49
Hackett, Daniel	45
Hackett, Ezekiel	49
Hackett, Joseph	49
Hackett, Samuel	49
Hadley, Samuel B., Corpl	39

AROOSTOOK WAR.

Name	Page
Hadley, William R.	46
Haines, Dudley L., Lieut.	65
Haines, George W.	27
Haines, Howard.	36
Haines, William S., Capt.	50
Hale, Albion K. P.	52
Hale, Alpheus R., Sergt.	44
Hale, Joseph W.	30
Hale, Reuben.	35
Hall, Arthur.	54
Hall, Charles.	66
Hall, Daniel B., Sergt.	70
Hall, Elisha.	66
Hall, George H.	69
Hall, Henry S.	38
Hall, Joseph.	49
Hall, Joshua T., Capt.	47
Hall, Josiah, Jr.	70
Hall, Kimball.	47
Hall, Lyman N.	45
Hall, Samuel P.	27
Hallett, Elias C., Sergt.	32
Ham, Joel.	49
Hamblet, Chas. R., Capt.	48
Hamilton, Alfred, Corpl.	49
Hamilton, Henry.	64
Hamilton, Hiram, Lieut.	49
Hamilton, Samuel.	58
Hamilton, Sumner.	60
Hamlin, Charles, Corpl.	26
Hamlin, Eleazer.	52
Hamlin, Elijah L.	22
Hamlin, Jesse.	71
Hammond, George W.	27
Hammond, George H.	55
Hammon, William P., Sergt.	38
Hanley, James R.	22
Hanson, Albert.	37
Hanson, Levi.	54
Hanscomb, Joseph.	71
Hanscomb, Nathaniel.	48
Harmon, Abial.	41
Harmon, Albert.	30
Harmon, Ephraim, Lieut.	30
Harmon, Edward.	42
Hardison, Sabin.	34
Hardison, Stephen, 2d.	34
Harding, Charles.	67
Harden, Isaac.	68
Hardin, Marshal.	54
Hardy, Asa.	47
Harridan, Washington F.	66
Harriman, Elias, Corpl.	48
Harriman, Ephraim E.	43
Harriman, Joab.	43
Harper, James C., Capt.	51
Harlow, Elbridge G.	66
Harris, Benjamin.	66
Harris, George.	30
Harris, Jairus.	40
Harris, William.	35
Hartford, James.	52
Harvey, Harrison.	28
Haskell, Andrew M.	58
Haskell, Charles.	58
Haskell, Daniel M., Sergt.	58
Haskell, David H., Capt.	52
Haskell, Greenleaf.	26
Haskell, John, Corpl.	66
Haskell, John T.	46
Haskell, Moses.	53
Hasselton, Joshua.	52
Hastings, Gideon A.	56
Hastings, Richard.	34
Hasty, James M.	30
Hasty, James, Jr., Sergt.	32
Hatch, Benjamin.	42
Hatch, William P.	60
Hathaway, Columbus.	51
Hawes, Christopher.	48
Hawes, Henry.	58
Hawes, Hiram, Corpl.	58
Hawes, Luther.	68
Hawes, William B., Cornet.	69
Hawkes, Edward P.	53
Hawkes, James R.	53
Hawkins, John F.	38
Hayden, Aaron, Jr.	22
Haynes, Hiram, Sergt.	37
Haynes, James M.	30
Haynes, Stephen P.	59
Hayward, James.	32
Heald, Arthur, Mus'n.	61
Healy, Moses, Jr.	32
Heath, Jacob.	50
Heath, John A., Mus'n.	70
Heath, John.	26
Heath, Joseph, Jr.	31
Hemmenway, Joseph D.	68
Henderson, Thomas H.	37
Herrick, Arthur.	43
Herrick, George S., Corpl.	60
Herrick, Jeremiah H.	54
Herrick, Laomi S., Corpl.	35
Herrick, Nathan F., Sergt.	43
Herrick, Otis W.	37
Herrick, Thomas A., Mus'n.	54
Herrick, Thomas C.	35
Herrick, William A.	24
Herrin, Bowman.	35
Herrin, Samuel.	26
Hersey, Cyrus, Lieut.	56
Hersom, John, 2d.	42
Hewes, Daniel.	35
Hewes, Stephen S.	61
Heyward, Mathew.	65
Heywood, Willmoth.	59
Hichborn, Nathan H.	69
Higgins, Abisha.	32
Higgins, Adoniram.	34
Higgins, Asa.	46
Higgins, Bradford.	60
Higgins, Elisha S.	65
Higgins, Jesse, Jr.	46
Higgins, Jesse.	54
Higgins, Jeremiah.	68
Higgins, Joseph M.	46
Higgins, Nehemiah.	34
Higgins, William.	55
Hill, Benjamin.	62
Hill, Daniel K.	45
Hill, Henry B.	36
Hills, Isaac, 2d.	42
Hills, Isaac, 2d., Sergt.	61
Hills, Jason.	61

INDEX. 83

Name	Page
Hill, Jotham	65
Hill, Leroy	46
Hill, William J.	56
Hilman, David	65
Hillman, Samuel	57
Hilton, William H.	55
Hinckley, Lorenzo	35
Hobbs, Abrah, Lieut.	62
Hodgdon, Allen	65
Hodgdon, Ebenezer	28
Hodgdon, George	39
Hodgdon, Joseph	59
Hodgdon, Moses	59
Hodgdon, Thomas	46
Hodges, Chas. E., Mus'n	27
Hodgkins, Philip, Corpl	34
Hodgkins, Thomas	61
Hodsdon, Chas. M.	57
Hodsdon, Isaac, Maj. Gen	22
Hodsdon, John L.	22
Hogan, William S.	68
Holbrook, Asa C.	65
Holbrook, Asa C.	65
Holbrook, Thomas W.	50
Holden, Columbus, Corpl.	52
Holman, John B., Sergt.	47
Holman, Merrill, Ens.	51
Holmes, James	32
Holmes, Stewart	53
Holmes, William	29
Holt, Abbot	31
Holt, Daniel G., Sergt.	31
Holt, Dudley B.	62
Holt, Erastus	51
Holt, Herman	51
Holt, Samuel H.	40
Holt, Seth	41
Holt, Stephen D.	70
Holtt, Samuel P.	54
Holyoke, Jacob, Corpl.	60
Homans, James S.	60
Homes, Ezra	48
Hopkins, Enoch	46
Hopkins, Samuel M.	70
Hopkins, Spencer, Mus'n	37
Hooper, Oliver P., Corpl.	65
Hor, Joseph	62
Hor, Nathan	62
Horne, Isaac	52
Horn, James	40
House, David B.	61
House, James L.	36
Houston, Samuel	60
Hovey, Manassah, S.	60
Hovey, Thomas, Lieut.	50
Howard, Amos	34
Howard, Charles A.	35
Howard, Cyril	42
Howard, Daniel	48
Howard, Daniel H.	57
Howe, Alvin	56
Howe, Henry L.	37
Howe, Phineas, Capt.	24
Howes, Edward	71
Hubbard, John H.	54
Huff, Benjamin W.	58
Huckins, Barzillai, Corpl.	48
Humphrey, Benjamin, Jr.	53
Hunt, Albert G.	57
Hunt, Albert G.	43
Hunt, Silas, Mus'n	50
Huntington, Benj. G.	44
Hunton, Wellington, Ens.	36
Huntress, Orin, Sergt.	51
Hurd, Manoah	60
Hutchins, Enos A.	47
Hutchins, Henry	36
Hutchins Jesse, Sergt.	41
Hutchins, Jesse	42
Hutchins, Silas	65
Hutchings, Joseph, Jr., Sergt.	64
Hutchinson, Benj. F.	70
Hutchinson, Ebenezer, Sergt.	47
Hutchinson, John, Lieut.	51
Hutchinson, Mark	30
Hutchinson, Stephen D.	66
Huxford, James, Capt.	54
Huxford, Lucius, Mus'n	54

I

Name	Page
Ingalls, Daniel	46
Ingalls, Jacob, Jr.	43
Ingalls, Moses, Jr.	59
Ingalls, Nahum H.	54
Ireland, Banjamin	57
Ireland, David G.	60
Irish, Abram M.	66
Irish, Daniel H., Corpl.	67
Irish, Edmund, Jr., Drum Maj.	24

J

Name	Page
Jackman, Aaron	55
Jackman, Sewall	49
Jackman, William C.	36
Jackson, Ezekiel C., Corpl.	35
Jackson, Oren	54
Jackson, Samuel, Corpl.	44
Jacobs, Benjamin F.	65
Jacobs, John	27
Jacobs, Rhodney, Corpl.	42
Jacques, William	29
James, Joseph	41
Jameson, William	68
Jaquith, John	71
Jaquith, Josiah	63
Jasper, Samuel B.	55
Jellison, David C., Sergt.	41
Jellison, David C., Sergt.	43
Jellison, Derry P.	40
Jennings, Abiather I.	47
Jennings, Charles	57
Jennings, Stephen D., Corpl.	57
Jenkins, Thomas	60
Jenness, John	35
Jewell, Elias L.	65
Jewett, Daniel T., Q. M.	22
Johnson, Albert	63
Johnson, Amasa, Mus'n	45
Johnson, Chancellor	32
Johnson, David	52
Johnson, Ephraim	60
Johnson, Haskell W.	24
Johnson, Kimball	54
Johnson, McKeen, Sergt.	53
Johnson, Robert	43
Johnson, Robert	57

	Page		Page
Johnson, Sanford	65	Kimball, Sabin H., Corpl	48
Johnson, William	59	Kimball, Thomas	54
Johnson, William L.	57	Kincaid, Samuel	33
Johnson, William M., Corpl	35	King, James, 2d	34
Johnson, William H., Corpl	55	Kingsley, Rufus	33
Johnson, William L.	43	Kinsman, John D., Capt	55
Johnson, William	43	Kirkpatrick, Alfred, Lieut	58
Jones, Charles, Jr	46	Kneeland, David	59
Jones, Charles, Ens	67	Kneeland, Ebenezer	52
Jones, Edson	45	Kneeland, Ephraim W	52
Jones, George	36	Knight, Elmere	56
Jones, Henry, Corpl	45	Knight, James	52
Jones, James	45	Knight, Lemuel, Mus'n	67
Jones, Lebbeus	54	Knight, Lorenzo	56
Jones, Lewis, Sergt	66	Knight, Moses	67
Jones, Nathaniel, Corpl	37	Knight, Samuel	58
Jones, Simeon H	67	Knight, Samuel	58
Jones, Solomon V., Corpl	37	Knight, Thaddeus R., Corpl	67
Jones, Stephen	40	Knight, Warren	46
Jones, William H	45	Knowles, Augustus	27
Jordan, Abel S	41	Knowles, Harrison	26
Jordan, Benjamin R	53	Knowles, Jonathan	37
Jordan, Joseph	59	Knowles, John	27
Jordan, Mial, Mus'n	39	Knowlton, Gilbert	41
Jordan, William	62	Knowlton, Joel	29
Joy, Hollis	64	Knowlton, John W	37
Joy, William	64	Knox, John	48
Judkins, Benjamin	59	Knox, Stephen	42
Judkins, Josiah A	31	Knox, Thomas J	37
Jumper, Charles, Corpl	57		
Jumper, Cyrus, Corpl	57	**L**	
Jumper, William	57	Lackey, Henry S., Sergt	69
		Ladd, Attilius, Sergt	48
K		Ladd, Harvey, Corpl	65
Katon, Alexander T., Sergt	50	Ladd, John C	58
Keene, Cyrus A	67	Ladd, Reuben	36
Keene, Gaius	45	Lamb, James B., Ens	44
Keisor, Francis C., Corpl	60	Lamb, James	47
Kelley, Charles	40	Lambert, Jesse	69
Kelley, Ebenezer	64	Lambert, Joseph	63
Kelley, Francis	33	Lamson, John	26
Kelley, George A	68	Lancaster, David	41
Kelley, John F	69	Lancaster, Royal	68
Kelliher, Joseph, Corpl	46	Lancaster, Valentine R	37
Kellier, William	33	Lander, William	32
Kemp, John	55	Lane, Barzillai W., Sergt	54
Kendal, Daniel G	31	Lane, Erastus, Corpl	54
Kendall, Robert P., Sergt	53	Lane, James	57
Kenerson, Bryant	51	Lane, John W	44
Kennison, George F	39	Lane, John W	59
Kennison, John R	67	Lane, Mathias	59
Kenney, Isaac S	54	Lane, Rufus K., Sergt	27
Kent, Ichabod, Sergt	46	Lankester, Solomon P	59
Keys, Oliver	51	Larrabee, Ammi	45
Keys, Otis	54	Larrabee, Hiram	48
Kidder, Augustus	51	Larrabee, Josiah A	37
Kilburn, Levi R	41	Larrabee, Simeon	37
Kildreth, Asa	67	Lassell, William	41
Kilgore, Moses H	31	Latham, Artemas	53
Kilgore, Thomas	63	Latham, J. Ezra	53
Kilton, William	33	Lawrence, Daniel	56
Kimball, David	52	Lawrence, Daniel	41
Kimball, Jacob	65	Lawrence, James P., Mus'n	29
Kimball, Jedediah	58	Lawrence, John N	41
Kimball, John	57	Lawrence, Roland	41
Kimball, Lewis	68	Lawrence, William, 2d	65
Kimball, Nathan, Corpl	44	Lawton, Daniel	27
Kimball, Reuben	39	Lawton, John	59

INDEX. 85

Name	Page
Leach, Ephraim O., Corpl.	32
Leach, Gideon.	51
Leach, Josiah B.	46
Leathers, Benjamin.	54
Leathers, Tuttle D.	48
Leathers, William W.	30
Leavitt, Eliphalet.	59
Leavitt, Hiram.	66
Leavitt, John.	57
Leavitt, Silas.	57
Lebroke, Hiram.	61
Lee, James.	48
Lee, William.	46
Leeman, Moses D.	27
Leighton, Almon.	64
Leighton, Harvey E.	58
Leighton, James.	29
Leighton, John.	64
Leighton, Lemuel.	36
Leighton, Samuel, Jr.	36
Leighton, Samuel P., Ord. Sergt.	43
Leighton, Samuel P., Q. M.	24
Leighton, Seaman.	33
Leighton, Seba F.	57
Leighton, Stephen, Jr., Capt.	57
Leighton, Thomas.	64
Leighton, Woodbury, Sergt.	64
Lervey, Samuel, Jr.	34
Leslie, Joseph, Sergt.	35
Lewis, Everett.	33
Lewis, James B.	44
Lewis, Thomas.	65
Libby, Benjamin F.	30
Libby, Benjamin, Jr.	65
Libbey, Benjamin.	67
Libby, Charles.	70
Libby, Cyrus J.	53
Libbey, Josiah.	31
Libby, John C.	69
Libby, Walter.	52
Libby, William.	52
Libby, William M.	63
Lincoln, George, Corpl.	41
Linnell, Enoch.	66
Linnell, Luther.	62
Liscomb, Gideon.	46
Little, William, Jr.	50
Little, William, Jr.	70
Littlefield, Charles.	39
Littlefield, Daniel S.	58
Littlefield, James, Sergt.	40
Littlefield, Robert.	60
Lock, Josiah R.	36
Logan, Charles R.	57
Logan, George P., Sergt.	43
Logan, George P.	57
Lombard, James A.	61
Lombard, Simon.	67
Longley, Asa.	40
Longley, David M.	30
Longley, Edward P.	57
Longley, William M.	65
Longfellow, George A., Sergt.	61
Longfellow, Newall.	68
Lopans, Abraham W.	34
Lord, Abram.	39
Lord, Horace.	59
Lord, Jeremiah, Ens.	24
Lord, John H.	65
Lord, Nathaniel.	62
Lord, Richard.	52
Lord, William.	36
Loring, George.	52
Lothrop, Elias L., Sergt.	28
Lothrop, Leonard.	51
Lothrop, Orman F.	48
Lougee, James.	58
Lovett, Alfred S.	59
Lovitt, Gardner.	55
Lovejoy, Azel.	47
Lovejoy, Christopher.	51
Lovejoy, David P., Sergt.	63
Lovejoy, Henry B.	62
Lovejoy, Joseph.	56
Lovejoy, Joseph C., Chaplain.	22
Lovejoy, Hubbard, Capt.	63
Low, Charles.	35
Low, Elijah O., Sergt.	61
Low, Lehi.	29
Lowell, Ebenezer.	54
Lowder, Jonathan, Lieut.	60
Luce, Freeman.	35
Luce, Hebron O., Sergt.	58
Luce, Oliver.	68
Luckings, Thomas P.	37
Ludden, Timothy, Capt.	56
Lufkin, Aaron H.	47
Lufkin, Lory C.	56
Lumbert, Enoch R., Capt.	58
Lundy, Sanford P.	65
Lunt, Isaac, Corpl.	61
Lunt, John S.	55
Lunt, Levi, Lieut.	38
Lyford, Fifield, Lieut.	58
Lynn, David.	26
Lyon, David.	26
Lyon, Ezra.	26
Lyon, George W.	50
Lyon, Peter.	44
Lyon, William.	27

M

Name	Page
Macomber, John C., Sergt.	46
Madden, Rufus.	33
Maddocks, Walter D.	48
Maker, Robert.	37
Mann, Thomas.	41
Mansel, Ira.	35
Mansfield, Ebenezer F., Sergt.	39
Mansfield, Stephen P.	45
Mariner, James H.	44
Marr, Foxwell C., Q. M.	22
Marr, H. S. P., Sergt.	63
Marson, Isaac.	45
Marshall, William.	52
Marston, Eben.	39
Marston, Henry.	39
Marston, Jasper, Sergt.	66
Marston, Samuel, Corpl.	31
Martin, Henry B.	40
Martin, John.	45
Martin, Lewis.	46
Mason, Andrew.	37
Mason, Broadstreet, Jr.	68
Mason, Ethan A.	70

	Page		Page
Mason, J. A. C.	68	Merrill, Josiah	67
Mason, Lawson, Corpl	56	Merrill, Lorenzo	66
Mason, Philip, Sergt.	67	Merrill, Rufus N.	30
Masterman, Daniel	56	Merrill, True	68
Masterman, Joseph N., Sergt.	51	Merrifield, Ivory	39
Mathews, William	54	Merryfield, Alvin, Corpl	59
Maxim, Banjamin, Lieut.	45	Merritt, Curtis	29
Maxim, George W., Capt.	60	Merritt, Uriah, Mus'n	64
Maxim, Jacob, Jr.	44	Messenger, Hazel, Corpl	35
Maxim, Thomas	44	Milliken, Benjamin	46
Maxfield, Eliphalet I., Capt.	59	Miller, David	61
Maxwell, John M., Sergt.	49	Miller, Eliphalet, Capt.	24
Maxwell, Moses	53	Miller, James, Jr.	61
Maxwell, William L., Sergt.	32	Miller, Jason	35
Maybury, Joshua	67	Miller, John E.	41
Mayhew, Abijah	38	Miller, Sewall	61
Mayhew, Asia, Corpl	38	Miles, Abram	58
Maynor, Moses	60	Miles, Josiah	59
Mayo, Enoch R.	35	Mills, Cyrus	31
Mayo, James	34	Mills, Ruel	42
Mayo, William H.	35	Mills, William H., Capt.	61
McCarthy, Charles	29	Millett, Chandler F., Sergt.	45
McCaslin, Amaziah N.	29	Millet, Samuel T.	38
McCaslin, Stephen J.	29	Millet, Samuel V.	35
McCausland, Charles	71	Minor, Dwight	50
McCausland, Thomas	61	Minor, Lyman	48
McCausland, William H.	65	Mitchell, Elijah S.	69
McCondray, Ephraim B.	60	Mitchell, Franklin	31
McCrillis, William H.	22	Mitchell, Francis B.	55
McDaniels, Dean	52	Mitchell, Henry	51
McFarland, David	49	Mitchell, Jason, Lieut.	67
McFarland, Geo. W., Corpl.	40	Mitchell, Jesse	28
McFarland, James	49	Mitchell, Joseph A.	68
McFarland, Moses, Ens	34	Mitchell, Nathaniel, Jr.	55
McGaffey, David, Jr., Sergt.	36	Mitchell, Nelson	35
McGrath, Theodore	32	Mitchell, Samuel	48
McIntire, Ephraim	67	Mitchell, Silas	56
McIntire, Philip	35	Montgomery, Henry	41
McIntire, Timothy, Corpl	39	Moody, Carlton P.	59
McIntosh, John	53	Moody, Charles	50
McKenney, Charles	50	Moody, Edlon D.	27
McKenney, Isaiah	60	Moody, John	50
McKenney, Silas	47	Moody, Lewis	50
McKenney, William	48	Moody, Rufus	59
McKinsey, Joseph D.	29	Moody, Sylvanus P.	66
McKusick, Francis	56	Moody, William B.	41
McLane, Daniel	54	Moor, Isaiah	34
McLure, James	29	Moore, Benjamin	70
McPheters, Josiah, Corpl	41	Moore, Daniel J.	42
MacPheters, Prentice R.	46	Moore, Ezekiel W.	46
McPheters, Samuel	59	Moore, Jere H., Sergt.	53
McRoy, Francis	33	Moore, John	61
McTosh, James G.	59	Moore, John	46
McTosh, William H.	59	Moore, Robert, Ens.	33
Mead, James	54	Moores, William	40
Mead, Jason	30	Morgan, Asa G.	46
Meader, William	68	Morgan, Edward	37
Melvin, Adorno L.	27	Morgan, Jesse	62
Merriam, Artemas	58	Morgan, John	59
Merrill, Ansel	51	Morgan, John	65
Merrill, Charles	66	Morgan, Solomon, Jr.	66
Merrill, Curtis B.	30	Morgan, Theophilus	26
Merrill, Cyrus	56	More, Eben P.	34
Merrill, Daniel	30	Morey, Solomon	40
Merrill, Ebenezer	71	Morrill, Frederic	59
Merrill, George W.	59	Morrill, Henry, Brig. Q. M.	22
Merrill, Hiram	66	Morrill, John S., Sergt.	27
Merrill, John	30	Morrill, Nicholas D.	45

INDEX. 87

	Page		Page
Morris, Abram, Lieut	70	Norton, Samuel, Jr	59
Morris, Benjamin	34	Norwood, Jonathan	34
Morris, William B	30	Norwood, Samuel	34
Morse, Isaac W	70	Noyes, Amos F., Capt	62
Morse, Nathan, Jr	62	Noyes, Calvin L	59
Morse, Nathan W	65	Noyes, Edward H	56
Morse, Samuel	36	Noyes, Ezra	47
Morse, Seth	56	Noyes, George	70
Morton, Daniel	31	Noyes, George, Sergt. Maj	24
Moshier, Davis	36	Noyes, Henry, Sergt	37
Moshier, Stephen	24	Noyes, Henry, Ord. Sergt	43
Moulton, Daniel, Sergt	60	Noyes, James C	38
Moulton, James M	63	Nugent, William	64
Moulton, Randall	69	Nutting, Asa	71
Moulton, Stephen C	58	Nute, John	58
Mower, Simeon C., Corpl	49	Nutter, Lemuel	34
Murch, Aaron, Jr	49		
Murch, Benjamin B., Mus'n	66	O	
Murch, Cyrus	46	Oakes, Ebenezer G	54
Murch, John L	46	Oaks, George	57
Murdock, Edmund	66	Ober, Nicholas	46
Murray, Reuben	65	O'Brien, Matthew	29
Murray, Samuel	69	Orcutt, John G., Corpl	70
Myrick, Amos S., Corpl	61	Ordway, Henry	39
Myrick, Nathaniel	40	Ordway, John	39
Myrick, Reuben	35	Orff, Simon	60
		O'Rooke, James	60
N		Osgood, Alva	41
Nash, Abner	64	Osgood, Charles S	39
Nash, James	53	Osgood, Fred P	54
Nash, John E	51	Osgood, Isaac	54
Nash, Levi	64	Overlock, Christopher	40
Nash, Stillman, Capt	64	Overlock, Martin	40
Nason, Jeremiah	66	Owen, Jefferson	63
Neal, Daniel	71		
Neal, William	58	P	
Nealley, Daniel D	69	Packard, Alfred	68
Nelson, John, Ens	48	Packard, Noah	66
Nelson, Joseph, Sergt	59	Packard, Reuben	42
Nelson, Oliver	52	Packard, Sewall	42
Nesmith, Isaac C	54	Packard, Sidney	26
Newbit, Alden	43	Page, Benjamin M., Sergt	48
Newcomb, Charles	41	Page, Charles R	27
Newcomb, Lowell	30	Page, David L	27
Newcomb, Peter B	61	Page, Dennis	53
Newcomb, Stillman	48	Page, Dustan	43
Newell, Samuel	55	Page, Ezekiel	53
Newingham, Nicholas	29	Page, Ezekiel	58
Newton, Estes	51	Page, Lewis	44
Newton, Jacob F	51	Page, Moses S., Sergt	41
Newton, James N	31	Page, Nathaniel	44
Nichols, Jerome, Fife Maj	24	Page, Nathaniel P., Q. M. Sergt.	24
Nichols, Joram, Mus'n	37	Page, Norman	60
Nickerson, Freeman	69	Page, Sewall, Corpl	42
Nickerson, Nathaniel	69	Paine, Brian	30
Nickerson, Shuber, Jr	60	Paine, George	40
Noble, Lorenzo H	62	Paine, Jacob	38
Noble, Nathan K., Sergt	62	Paine, James	71
Norcross, Israel	35	Paine, John	61
Norcross, Nathaniel, Maj	22	Palmer, Charles, Adjt	22
Norris, Alden W	67	Palmer, Daniel	57
Norris, Benjamin	36	Palmer, Manley	28
Norris, George	34	Palmer, Thomas F	36
Norris, Trafton	67	Palmer, William H	40
Norton, Elijah	58	Parcher, Loren, Corpl	28
Norton, Joshua W., Corpl	29	Park, Roderick R	41
Norton, Joseph F	50	Parker, Amasa W	54
Norton, Russell	65	Parker, Henry D	33

	Page		Page
Parker, Luther	33	Peterson, Israel R	38
Parker, Jonathan	51	Pettengill, Jason	28
Parker, William	38	Pettengill, John	55
Parsons, Edwin	55	Philbrick, John, Colonel	22
Parsons, John	60	Philbrick, John R	36
Parret, Stilman	33	Philbrick, Lucius	67
Partridge, John	26	Philbrick, Oliver S	36
Patch, Jonathan	27	Philbrook, Jason R	40
Pattee, Daniel, Corpl	68	Philbrook, Luther G	37
Pattee, James, Mus'n	68	Phillips, Edmund	44
Pattee, Stephen B	61	Pickard, Amos, Lieut	24
Patridge, Francis	54	Pickering, Isaac H	57
Patten, Charles	41	Pickett, James	29
Patten, Francis B	33	Pierce, Asa	51
Patten, James R	58	Pierce, Jonathan W	71
Patten, Levi B	61	Pierce, Samuel	41
Patten, Michael H	54	Pike, Dudley	45
Patten, Michael L	33	Pike, George W	30
Patten, Nathaniel R	58	Pike, Henry	37
Patten, Pickering, Sergt	29	Pike, Prescott S	62
Patterson, Amasa T., Corpl	37	Pike, William, Mus'n	30
Patterson, Benjamin	35	Pilley, John Penn, Sergt	54
Patterson, Frederick A	37	Pilsbury, Peter	46
Patterson, Isaac	69	Pinkham, Charles	71
Patterson, James G., Corpl	60	Pinkham, Joseph	51
Patterson, James	30	Pinkham, Reuben, Jr	71
Patterson, John	37	Pinkham, Uriah	64
Patterson, Lewis A	37	Pinkham, William	27
Patterson, Samuel	60	Pinkham, William	42
Peabody, Benjamin, Jr	62	Pishon, Hiram, Lieut	63
Peabody, Joshua	29	Pitcher, Jonathan, Jr	57
Peacock, James, Corpl	65	Pitts, Abner, Jr., Sergt	50
Peacock, Solomon	65	Pitts, Emerson, Mus'n	51
Peacock, William	65	Place, William	26
Peare, Moses	49	Plummer, Bidfield, Lieut	69
Pearl, Isaac	39	Plummer, Fellars	29
Pearl, John E	39	Plummer, George H., Corpl	55
Pearl, Josiah, Mus'n	32	Plummer, John A	61
Peasley, Enoch	60	Pollard, Ezekiel	38
Peasley, Nathan G., Corpl	29	Pollard, Hiram A., Capt	66
Peavey, Hiram	40	Pollard, Sylvanus	38
Peavey, Jonathan	40	Pollard, William	66
Peavey, Joseph C	32	Pomroy, Francis N	69
Peavey, Joseph	32	Pond, Daniel, Jr	38
Peavey, William	32	Pool, Calvin	38
Pendleton, James H	69	Pool, Henry O	36
Pennell, Charles	55	Poor, William, Jr	45
Pennell, Thomas, Mus'n	30	Porter, Charles	43
Perkins, Barzillai	65	Porter, Charles	65
Perkins, Enoch	24	Porter, Charles C., Surgeon	22
Perkins, Ephraim M	54	Porter, David	68
Perkins, Gordon	70	Porter, Ezekiel L., Corpl	38
Perkins, Nathaniel	35	Porter, William	65
Perkins, Oliver, Sergt	56	Pote, Robert P	37
Perkins, Robert	58	Potter, Benjamin	71
Perkins, Stover	59	Potter, Elijah R	49
Perkins, Thomas	69	Potter, James W	50
Perkins, William	27	Potter, James S	37
Perry, Clark	61	Powers, William H., Sergt	39
Perry, David	34	Pratt, Alanson S	62
Perry, Josiah W	64	Pratt, Andrew	62
Perry, Joseph, Capt	65	Pratt, Benjamin	60
Perry, Levi M., Mus'n	58	Pratt, George	60
Perry, Ozias B	64	Pratt, Horatio	43
Persons, Elisha, 2d, Corpl	69	Pratt, Horatio	57
Peters, Daniel S., Ord. Sergt	43	Pratt, John	59
Peterson, Benjamin, Jr	45	Pratt, Joseph	55

INDEX.   89

	Page		Page
Pratt, Simon, Sergt	26	Richards, Almon	61
Pray, Edmund, Jr	26	Richards, Curtis C	53
Pray, John, Sergt	40	Richards, Francis	30
Pray, Reuben	42	Richards, Josiah	59
Preble, Galen O	33	Richardson, Atwell, Corpl	45
Prentiss, Henry E., Capt	22	Richardson, Bemis	67
Prescott, Eli L	49	Richardson, Darius	62
Prescott, James	35	Richardson, Enoch	29
Prescott, Joseph N., Div. Insp.	22	Richardson, Erastus H	34
Prescott, Stephen A	49	Richardson, George, Corpl	63
Priest, George W	32	Richardson, George	68
Priest, Joseph	41	Richardson, John, Jr	36
Prim, John	70	Richardson, Joseph	34
Prime, Hiram	42	Richardson, Joshua W	55
Proctor, William, Sergt	30	Richardson, Leander	34
Puffer, John	40	Richardson, Lyman	62
Pugsley, Abraham	56	Richardson, Oliver	39
Pullen, Granville D	32	Richardson, Samuel H	36
Purington, Fred	53	Richardson, Silas, Mus'n	32
Purington, Joseph C	30	Richmond, Alanson	66
		Richmond, Solomon	66
		Ricker, Bradford W	45
Q			
Quimby, John, Lieut	58	Ricker, Harris	28
Quint, Ivory	27	Ricker, Ivory	32
		Ricker, John	57
R		Ricker, Joseph, Jr	32
Radford, Lincoln, Sergt	55	Ricker, Samuel	68
Ramsdell, Harvey	27	Ricker, Simeon E., Corpl	68
Ramsdell, Oren A	63	Rider, Isaac	48
Ramsdell, William H	60	Rideout, Luther, Sergt	58
Rand, Marshall H	37	Riggs, Wilmot	60
Rand, Nahum	56	Rines, Allen	60
Randall, Asa	36	Rines, John	32
Randall, Samuel, 3d	52	Rinds, Joseph S	37
Randlett, James N., Sergt	49	Ring, David	67
Randlett, Samuel M	49	Ring, John	61
Rankins, Enoch	56	Ripley, David R., Capt	67
Rankins, Perley	56	Ripley, Orison, Colonel	22
Ray, George A., Corpl	47	Robbins, Oliver, 2d	38
Ray, Judson	64	Roberts, Benjamin	54
Ray, Washington	66	Roberts, Cyrus	37
Raymond, Ralph T	63	Robert, Charles	53
Raymond, Solomon	51	Roberts, Nathaniel E	48
Raymond, Thomas	41	Roberts, Samuel	40
Rawson, Ebenezer G., Div. Q. M.,	22	Roberts, Winslow	54
Rawson, Horace	67	Robertson, Richard, Jr	69
Rea, John, Jr	70	Robey, John, Jr	26
Record, Asa	56	Robie, Joseph, Corpl	71
Record, Benjamin H	66	Robinson, Alexander	66
Reed, Amaziah	51	Robinson, Alden	38
Reed, Ezra D., Sergt	34	Robinson, Alfred	52
Reed, George B	35	Robinson, Charles N. B	69
Reed, Harvey	35	Robinson, David	36
Reed, Jeremiah	58	Robinson, Elijah	53
Reed, Thomas	71	Robinson, Francis F	67
Remick, Benjamin	65	Robinson, Jonathan E., Sergt	36
Remick, Warren I., Q. M. Sergt.,	24	Robinson, John J	64
Remmick, Philip	46	Robinson, William	34
Reynolds, James	29	Roff, John	64
Reynolds, William, Sergt	54	Roff, Hiram	64
Rich, Aaron W	62	Rogers, George W	48
Rich, Franklin	54	Rogers, Gustavus, Corpl	53
Rich, John	46	Rogers, James	61
Rich, Luther	47	Rogers, William G	59
Rich, Oliver T	54	Rogers, William	66
Rich, Peter J	48	Rolf, David F	30
Rich, Reuben, Jr	56	Rollins, Axel I	51

	Page		Page
Rollins, Eliphalet, Corpl	50	Sawyer, Francis O	30
Rollins, Greenwood, Sergt	42	Sawyer, Henry K	57
Rollins, Joseph	26	Sawyer, James H	37
Rollins, Owen S	37	Sawyer, Jabez, Corpl	38
Rollins, T. W	50	Sawyer, John F., Lieut	53
Rose, Alden	66	Sawyer, John E., Sergt	28
Rose, Elbridge G	43	Sawyer, Nathaniel K., Sergt	37
Rose, Emerson	45	Sawyer, Nathaniel, Capt	68
Rose, George	32	Sawyer, Reuben A	53
Rose, Harrison, Corpl	28	Scammons, Dudley	34
Rose, Joseph	35	Scammons, Samuel, Sergt	34
Rose, Joseph	48	Scott, John	59
Rounds, Ephraim	38	Seaman, Alfred	40
Rounds, George	30	Seaver, William H., Corpl	62
Row, Solomon P., Mus'n	41	Seavey, James	55
Rowe, Benjamin, Ens	54	Sedgely, Edward, Corpl	28
Rowe, Learned	54	Segee, George W	69
Rowell, Joseph P., Corpl	49	Seiders, Charles A	65
Royal, Rufus S	47	Severance, George W	57
Royal, Silas	48	Severance, Seth	48
Royal, Tristram	64	Shackley, John	47
Royal, William	67	Shackleton, John	58
Ruggles, Paul, Surgeon	22	Shaw, Cyrus	62
Rumble, John, Corpl	33	Shaw, Edwardus	55
Rundlett, Jacob, Corpl	36	Shaw, John	35
Runnels, John S	58	Shaw, John	33
Russ, James, Sergt	56	Shaw, John M., Mus'n	57
Russ, Jesse	60	Shaw, Luthur H	57
Russell, George, Sergt	52	Shaw, John M., Drum Major	24
Russell, Moses B	67	Shaw, Nathan S	35
Russell, Philo E	51	Shaw, Nelson	30
Russell, Samuel B	27	Shea, Michael, Lieut	64
Ryerson, Job, Sergt	67	Sheet, Samuel	41
		Shepherd, Joseph R	65
S		Shepherd, William	48
Saben, John	26	Shepley, David	61
Safford, Calvin, Corpl	57	Shepley, Daniel	43
Safford, Hiram, Sergt	57	Shepley, Daniel C	61
Safford, John	57	Sherburn, William, Jr	60
Safford, Micah, Corpl	26	Shirley, Christopher	37
Safford, Simeon, Jr	57	Shirley, William	68
Salisbury, Calvin	46	Shorey, David	60
Sampson, Amos	52	Shorey, Henry A	32
Sampson, Darius	57	Shuman, John	37
Sampson, George R	48	Shuman, Simon	37
Sampson, Nathaniel, Corpl	62	Sias, Moses P	36
Sanborn, James	59	Sibley, Abram	60
Sands, Isaac	30	Sibley, Henry	48
Sanders, Benjamin C., Corpl	48	Sibley, Peter, Jr.,	32
Sanders, Edward	46	Sidelinger, Samuel	68
Sanders, Richard	46	Simmons, Charles, Ens	26
Sargent, Darius	35	Simons, Salon S	22
Sargent, Henry	64	Simpson, Benjamin	31
Sargent, John, Jr	22	Simpson, Daniel F	31
Sargent, John	64	Simpson, Jacob	41
Saunders, Jacob P., Ens	24	Simpson, John	31
Saunders, Nathaniel	43	Simpson, Joseph	31
Saunders, Silas	54	Simpson, Wells	48
Savage, Daniel, 2d	26	Sinclair, Benjamin	33
Sawtelle, Charles K	42	Sinclair, Joseph P	40
Sawtelle, Edwin	51	Sinclair, William	29
Sawtelle, Zalmon, Sergt	42	Skillings, William	53
Sawyer, Alfred	55	Skinner, Albert	58
Sawyer, Asa	60	Skinner, Justin	29
Sawyer, Benjamin	34	SkofField, Richard T	67
Sawyer, Daniel G	68	Small, Elbridge G. W	29
Sawyer, Ethan A	30	Small, James, 2d	33

INDEX. 91

Name	Page
Small, Joseph L.	55
Small, Nathan M.	55
Smart, Charles L.	59
Smart, Ira, Sergt.	67
Smart, John B.	37
Smart, Reuben S., Capt.	69
Smith, Alexander.	68
Smith, Amos.	54
Smith, Amos.	30
Smith, Andrew.	33
Smith, Archibald, Mus'n.	29
Smith, Augustus W.	68
Smith, Benjamin, Sergt.	34
Smith, Benjamin R.	70
Smith, Charles.	36
Smith, Christopher.	60
Smith, Ephraim P.	56
Smith, Etsil G., Mus'n.	56
Smith, Gardner.	58
Smith, George M.	67
Smith, George K., Sergt.	47
Smith, Gorham.	35
Smith, Gustavus W.	68
Smith, Hartson.	32
Smith, Henry, Sergt. Maj.	24
Smith, Isaac, Corpl.	34
Smith, James, Major.	24
Smith, James S. F.	49
Smith, John P.	58
Smith, John O.	63
Smith, Joseph, Sergt.	44
Smith, Joseph B.	70
Smith, John.	36
Smith, Madison.	51
Smith, Matthias, Mus'n.	36
Smith, Moses.	29
Smith, Orrington, Mus'n.	54
Smith, Otis.	68
Smith, Peter B.	55
Smith, Peter.	56
Smith, Rufus, Mus'n.	40
Smith, Russell.	29
Smith, Seth E.	31
Smith, Samuel.	22
Smith, Simon.	38
Smith, Sumner.	61
Smith, Sumner, Mus'n.	27
Smith, Taylor.	65
Smith, Thomas.	59
Smith, Thomas J., Sergt.	33
Smith, William.	53
Smith, William W., Corpl.	60
Snell, Albion, K. P.	55
Snow, David.	44
Snow, Henry.	57
Snow, Jesse, Sergt.	61
Snow, Kenney, Corpl.	41
Snow, Richard.	37
Snow, William C.	41
Snowman, John.	70
Somersby, Jacob.	46
Soule, Benjamin.	45
Southard, John, Jr.	41
Southwick, William.	32
Spaulding, Benjamin F.	56
Spaulding, Sidney.	38
Spear, Charles, Jr., Corpl.	44
Spencer, Samuel.	41
Spencer, Samuel, Corpl.	70
Spiller, Alpheus.	53
Spooner, Asa, Sergt.	57
Sprague, Charles S.	40
Sprague, Edmund.	65
Sprague, Henry A.	57
Spratt, Dudley D.	35
Springer, Leamon S.	33
Springer, Samuel, Mus'n.	34
Springer, Samuel.	34
Springer, Stephen C.	61
Springer, William.	34
Stacy, William H.	50
Stafford, Edward B.	69
Stain, John D.	36
Standish, Ellis, Jr.	62
Stanford, Alvan.	65
Stanley, George W.	27
Stanley, John.	45
Staple, Joseph.	53
Staples, John H.	39
Staples, Joshua.	70
Staples, Norris.	68
Starbird, Levi.	63
Starbird, Luther.	49
Starbird, Watson R.	51
Stavers, Charles.	40
Stearns, Absalom.	52
Stearns, David, Jr.	69
Stearns, Timothy.	52
Stephens, George A.	37
Stephens, James.	46
Stephens, Nathan.	68
Stephens, Nathan G.	42
Stetson, Benjamin F.	28
Stetson, Caleb.	65
Stetson, David.	66
Stetson, Henry.	42
Stetson, Nahum.	54
Stetson, Nathaniel.	28
Stevens, Ansel, Corpl.	62
Stevens, Benjamin W.	47
Stevens, Edward P.	55
Stevens, Edmund.	39
Stevens, Francis.	51
Stevens, George A.	61
Stevens, Hiram.	61
Stevens, Hiram B.	50
Stevens, Howard.	35
Stevens, James W., Corpl.	30
Stevens, John.	36
'Stevens, Joseph C., Div. Insp.	22
Stevens, Lora B., Lieut.	28
Stevens, Luther.	33
Stevens, Pillsbury, Ens.	64
Stevens, Samuel.	36
Stevens, Thomas H.	64
Stevens, William.	62
Stevens, William C.	48
Stevens, William H., Corpl.	33
Steward, Temple C.	29
Stewart, Frederic, Mus'n.	40
Stewart, George.	33
Stewart, Henry L., Ens.	61
Stewart, James H., Sergt.	40
Stewart, Samuel, Jr.	39

AROOSTOOK WAR.

Name	Page
Stiles, Asa L.	60
Stiles, Enoch, Corpl.	47
Stiles, Isaac.	45
Stimpson, Edwin E.	37
Stinchfield, Daniel L.	35
Stinson, Horatio N.	41
Stinson, Joseph C.	41
Stinson, Samuel F., Corpl.	69
Stinson, Waterman.	58
Stinson, William B.	69
Stockbridge, John C., Ens.	47
Stockin, Benjamin, Capt.	24
Stoddard, Christopher.	71
Stone, Alonzo.	52
Stone, Harrison, Mus'n.	26
Stone, Kendall H. K., Lieut.	44
Stone, Nathaniel, Lieut.	39
Storer, Albert, Sergt.	36
Storer, Horace.	39
Stover, Nathaneal, Corpl.	64
Stover, Sylvanus.	64
Strout, Alonzo.	53
Stowell, Elias.	67
Straw, Robert C.	70
Strickland, Alpheus W., Sergt.	31
Strout, David.	45
Strout, David P.	30
Strout, Ephraim.	64
Strout, George.	64
Strout, Horace.	33
Strout, Hooper D., Sergt.	53
Strout, John.	64
Strout, William.	64
Stuart, Amos C.	71
Stubbs, Cyrus.	70
Stubbs, James.	41
Stubbs, Lorenzo D.	28
Stubbs, Timothy.	69
Sturdevant, Francis J.	61
Sturdivant, Lott.	51
Sturtevant, Benj. B., Sergt.	67
Sturtevant, Curtis.	57
Sturtevant, Thomas.	38
Swan, Benjamin P.	22
Swan, Hiram.	35
Swan, Jacob, Mus'n.	35
Swan, John, Mus'n.	35
Swan, Nathan A., Lieut.	34
Swan, Nathaniel.	35
Swan, Orrin B.	56
Sweat, Jesse P., Surgeon Mate.	22
Sweetser, Daniel.	55
Swett, Alfred.	30
Swett, Henry L.	37
Swett, Jacob P.	41
Swett, Nathan H.	53
Swett, Roswell.	46
Swett, Stephen, Corpl.	36
Swetland, Nathan, Corpl.	56
Swift, William A., Corpl.	37
Sylvester, Elijah.	35
Sylvester, Joseph T.	61

T

Name	Page
Tabberts, Jeremiah.	29
Tabberts, John, 2d.	29
Tabberts, Otis.	29
Tabberts, Samuel H.	29
Taintor, Alsworth.	47
Tapley, Timothy C.	41
Tarr, John, Corpl.	56
Tarbox, Ephraim.	38
Tarbox, Hanson.	62
Tarbox, William, Adjt.	22
Taylor, Dean.	39
Taylor, Elias, 3d.	42
Taylor, Elijah.	70
Taylor, George W., Corpl.	31
Taylor, James.	65
Taylor, John B.	42
Tebbetts, Elijah, Mus'n.	45
Tebbetts, James.	63
Thayer, Ebenezer.	62
Thayer, Simon.	55
Thayer, Solomon.	51
Thayer, Solomon.	42
Thayer, Willard B., Mus'n.	42
Thoms, Harrison G. O.	57
Thoms, Peter A.	28
Thomas, Elbridge G.	51
Thomas, John W.	44
Thomas, Spofford P., Corpl.	46
Thompson, Alonzo.	5
Thompson, Emery.	54
Thompson, Hannibal, Sergt.	45
Thompson, Jeremiah.	61
Thompson, John, Corpl.	66
Thompson, John N., Sergt.	31
Thompson, Phineas.	39
Thompson, Samuel.	39
Thompson, Tobias.	70
Thorndike, Charles, Corpl.	54
Thorndike, Francis, Lieut.	54
Thornton, Wm. Jr., Sergt.	50
Thurston, Elem.	38
Thurlow, Leonard, Corpl.	56
Tibbetts, Andrew.	71
Tilton, Joseph.	48
Timberlake, Silas.	51
Tinkham, David W., Corpl.	32
Tinney, Otis.	29
Titcomb, William.	55
Tobbin, John.	58
Tobey, Curtis.	32
Tobey, Harrison.	65
Tobey, Wm. A., Lieut.	66
Tobin, Joseph, Jr.	51
Tobin, Mathew.	38
Tomlinson, Paul.	58
Toothaker, Ebenezer, Sergt.	71
Torrance, Levi S.	60
Torrance, Samuel S.	60
Tosh, William A.	59
Tower, Levi.	41
Towle, Elbridge G., Sergt.	65
Towle, Henry, Corpl.	30
Towle, Henry W.	42
Towle, Hiram, Mus'n.	42
Towle, John.	57
Towle, Thomas I., Corpl.	59
Towne, Eli.	61
Townsend, James.	53
Townsend, Joshua.	42
Townsend, Reuben, Sergt.	51

INDEX.   93

Name	Page
Townsend, William	46
Tourtilotte, Elisha	46
Tourtilotte, Joshua	46
Tozier, Benjamin F.	43
Tozier, Benjamin F.	57
Tozier, Thurston H., Corpl.	32
Tozier, William P.	32
Tracey, Darius O.	64
Tracey, Wheeler	64
Tracey, William	64
Tracy, Israel	59
Trask, Asa, Corpl.	50
Trask, James, Mus'n	26
Trask, Samuel	26
Trask, Samuel	42
Trask, William	48
Treadwell, James	69
Trevett, Samuel S	41
Treworgy, Albert, Ens.	46
Treworgy, Charles D	57
Treworgy, George	46
Treworgy, Solomon I., Sergt.	46
Triggs, Augustine	35
Tripp, Jacob	53
Tripp, James S.	31
True, Benjamin	53
True, Whittier, Sergt.	65
Trumbull, Foster	56
Trundy, Levi	69
Tubs, Elias A	45
Tuck, Jesse G., Sergt.	36
Tuck, Joseph, 2d	36
Tuck, Samuel, 2d, Corpl.	36
Tucker, David, Corpl.	51
Tucker, Elbridge	47
Tucker, Isaac	57
Tucker, Isaac N., Lieut. Col.	22
Tucker, John	29
Tuckerman, John	30
Tuell, Alonzo	67
Tuptle, Isaac	38
Turner, Alexander	66
Turner, Edwin, Sergt.	49
Turner, Josiah M.	53
Turner, Patrick	29
Turner, William	40
Tuttle, Isaac	58
Tuttle, John H., Corpl.	53
Twitchell, Asa C.	68
Twitchell, Milton, Sergt.	43
Twitchell, Milton	57
Twitchell, Ozman	56
Tyler, James	69

U

Name	Page
Uran, Elbridge G., Corpl.	34

V

Name	Page
Varney, John, Jr.	38
Varney, Paul, Q. M.	22
Varnum, Benjamin	46
Varnum, Samuel	46
Varrill, Lewis	66
Veriel, William, 3d	55
Verrill, William	69
Vickery, Joel, Sergt.	60
Vincent, Willard	35
Virgin, Stephen	47

W

Name	Page
Wade, Samuel, Corpl.	42
Wadleigh, Azariah	35
Wadleigh, Eli	40
Waire, Lyman, Sergt.	63
Walcott, Elmer B.	65
Waite, Rathons B., Mus'n	47
Wakefield, Paul P.	40
Wallace, Joseph	64
Wallon, Alexander D.	48
Walker, Aaron H.	35
Walker, Amasa R., Lieut.	48
Walker, Daniel	56
Walker, David, Col.	22
Walker, James, Capt.	24
Walker, Jason H.	31
Walker, Orrin	39
Walker, Otis	67
Walker, Samuel F.	61
Walker, William, Corpl.	27
Walker, William, Corpl.	31
Walker, William B.	57
Walker, William B., Sergt.	70
Ward, Calvin	40
Wardwell, Burnham	57
Wardwell, Isaac	52
Wardwell, Ira	57
Warren, Amos G.	55
Warren, Enoch S.	49
Warren, George D.	39
Warren, Henry, Q. M.	22
Warren, Ichabod, Corpl.	39
Warren, James	58
Warren, John	56
Warren, John, Sergt.	71
Warton, Joshua	59
Washburn, Ira	48
Washburn, Peleg	57
Waterman, Jacob, Corpl.	66
Watson, James H.	36
Watson, Joseph	53
Watson, Lewis, Surg. Mate	22
Watts, Samuel	54
Webb, Asa D., Sergt.	64
Webb, Daniel	52
Webb, Edward	54
Webb, Thomas	48
Webber, George B.	35
Webster, Daniel, Sergt.	58
Webster, Nathan	27
Webster, Richard, Jr.	58
Webster, S. S., Sergt.	26
Weeks, James, Jr., Sergt.	45
Weeks, Napoleon	45
Weeks, R. I.	63
Weeks, Stephen, Corpl.	39
Welch, Thomas	55
Wells, Lewis	26
Wentworth, Cyrus	45
Wentworth, George	55
Wentworth, John	34
Wentworth, Jonah	46
Wentworth, Nathaniel S.	40
Wentworth, William	56
West, James	48
West, John	58
West, Samuel	69
Weston, Joseph	67

	Page		Page
Weston, Zachariah	52	Williams, Miles	65
Weymouth, David	55	Williams, Shuber N	60
Weymouth, John	60	Williams, William	63
Weymouth, Mark G	59	Wilson, Charles	66
Weymouth, Robert H	61	Wilson, Jesse	26
Weymouth, Timothy H., Ens	53	Willson, John S., Ens	30
Whales, John	39	Wilson, John	46
Wheelden, Peter	35	Wilson, William F	37
Wheeler, David, Sergt	28	Wing, Alexander	49
Wheeler, Zenas, Sergt	29	Wing, B. C	63
Whitaker, Andrew	34	Wing, Charles H., Capt	70
Whitaker, Oren	34	Wing, George W	44
Whitcomb, Eben	37	Wing, Llewellyn, Mus'n	63
Whitcomb, Sewall	32	Wing, R. M	63
Whitcomb, Thomas	32	Wingate, George	33
Whitmore, John	33	Winship, Albert	67
Whitman, Harrison, Sergt	38	Winslow, Andrew C	57
Whitman, Barza	66	Winslow, Barnabas	66
Whitmore, Alanson M., Mus'n	38	Winslow, Eli	57
Whitmore, Cyprian	38	Winslow, Luther P	67
Whitmore, William C	51	Winslow, Oliver	30
Whittemore, George	57	Winter, John	47
Whittemore, Nelson	48	Witham, Jacob	56
Whittemore, Simon	48	Witham, John	60
White, Fred S	53	Witham, Pelatiah	39
White, George	64	Witham, Pelatiah	56
White, Joel, Jr	67	Witt, William P	62
White, John	51	Wood, Benson D	41
White, John, 2d	51	Wood, Borden	52
White, Nathaniel	40	Wood, Daniel, Q. M	22
White, Phanuel, Corpl	51	Woods, George W	36
White, Robert	53	Wood, John P., Lieut	37
White, Samuel, 3d	56	Woods, Sampson	36
White, Stillman S	33	Wood, Samuel, Jr., Maj	22
White, Stephen	60	Wood, Stephen	39
White, Thomas A	33	Wood, William	51
White, Tilley	64	Woodbury, George B	53
Whitney, Asa B	29	Woodbury, Nathan P	55
Whitney, Ephraim	33	Woodcock, George, Ens	42
Whitney, Levi, Jr	30	Woodcock, Hannibal H	44
Whitten, Amos, Corpl	29	Woodman, Ariel L	52
Whitten, Harris	64	Woodman, Asa	61
Whitten, Joseph	30	Woodman, Samuel M., Sergt	44
Whittier, Amasa	58	Woodman, William	32
Whittier, Charles	35	Woodward, Israel W., Lieut	71
Whittier, Elias	37	Woodward, John	48
Whittier, Jonathan	27	Woodward, Thomas	29
Whittier, Porter, Jr	58	Worcester, Lothrop, Sergt	30
Whittier, True, Sergt	65	Wormell, Cyrus, Sergt. Maj	24
Whittier, William H., Corpl	44	Wormell, Hiram, Sergt	56
Wiggins, Ephraim	26	Worster, Isaac, Jr	29
Wiggin, James M	27	Worster, John, Jr	29
Wight, Joseph R	31	Worster, Mark	29
Wight, Milton M	49	Worster, Moses, Jr., Corpl	29
Wilbur, John	55	Worster, William, Ens	29
Wiley, Charles	61	Worthin, Isaac	37
Wilkenson, Levi M	48	Worthing, William P	54
Willard, Rufus	57	Wright, John	26
Wille, Andrew	33	Wright, Nathan	53
Wille, Ephraim, Sergt	33	Wright, Thomas	29
Willey, Amos P	29	Wright, Thomas, Ens	24
Willey, Daniel	60	Wyman, Charles	32
Willey, Enoch	64	Wyman, Charles, Sergt	43
Willey, James B., Sergt	63	Wyman, Charles	57
Willey, William	35	Wyman, James E	32
Williams, Bela	31	Wyman, James	32
Williams, George	34		

INDEX. 95

Y

Name	Page	Name	Page
Yeaton, Daniel B.	56	Young David	59
Yeaton, Phineas, Jr.	27	Young, David, 2d	64
York, Charles E.	55	Young, Edwin	46
York, Ebenezer	31	Young, Ellis	46
York, Hiram, Sergt.	68	Young, Francis	60
York, Isaac J.	31	Young, George. Jr., Corpl.	65
York, John	52	Young, Henry, Mus'n	67
York, John A., Sergt.	68	Young, Hiram	47
York, Joseph, Sergt.	68	Young, James	31
York, Randall	31	Young, James	61
York, Rufus	68	Young, Jacob	64
York, Solomon, Sergt.	35	Young, John	26
York, William L.	53	Young, Joseph D.	68
Young, Albert R.	48	Young, Kendall	64
Young, Alfred	54	Young, Moses H., Lieut. Col.	22
Young, Atwood F. W.	53	Young, Winthrop	34
Young, Charles, Jr., Ens.	67	Young, William L.	37
Young, David	64	Young, William	53

www.ingramcontent.com/pod-product-compliance
Lightning Source LLC
Chambersburg PA
CBHW071159090426
42736CB00012B/2382